# FORKLIFT
# INSPECTION CHECKLIST BOOK

Company Name: _____

Dates Used:_____

Notes:_____

_____

_____

_____

_____

_____

_____

Date: _____ Shift: _____

Truck Number:_____ Electric:____ Internal Combustion:____

Hour Meter Start:_____ End:_____ Total Hours:_____

Check any defective item and explain in the notes section below:

| | | | |
|---|---|---|---|
| | Accelerator | | Hour Meter |
| | Alarms | | Hydraulic Controls |
| | Battery Connector | | Lights - Head and Tail |
| | Battery - Discharge Indicator | | Lights - Warning |
| | Belt | | Mast |
| | Brakes - Parking | | Oil Leaks |
| | Brakes - Service | | Oil Pressure |
| | Cables | | Overhead Guard |
| | Engine Oil Level | | Radiator Level |
| | Forks | | Safety Equipment |
| | Fuel | | Steering |
| | Gauges | | Tires |
| | Horn | | Unusual Noises |
| | Hoses | | Other _____ |

Notes:_____

_____

_____

_____

_____

_____

_____

_____

_____

Operator's Name:_____

Operator's Signature:_____

Supervisor's Name:_____

Supervisor's Signature:_____

Date: _____ Shift: _____

Truck Number:_____ Electric:____ Internal Combustion:____

Hour Meter Start:_____ End:_____ Total Hours:_____

Check any defective item and explain in the notes section below:

| | | | |
|---|---|---|---|
| | Accelerator | | Hour Meter |
| | Alarms | | Hydraulic Controls |
| | Battery Connector | | Lights - Head and Tail |
| | Battery - Discharge Indicator | | Lights - Warning |
| | Belt | | Mast |
| | Brakes - Parking | | Oil Leaks |
| | Brakes - Service | | Oil Pressure |
| | Cables | | Overhead Guard |
| | Engine Oil Level | | Radiator Level |
| | Forks | | Safety Equipment |
| | Fuel | | Steering |
| | Gauges | | Tires |
| | Horn | | Unusual Noises |
| | Hoses | | Other _____ |

Notes:_____

_____

_____

_____

_____

_____

_____

_____

_____

Operator's Name:_____

Operator's Signature:_____

Supervisor's Name:_____

Supervisor's Signature:_____

Date: _____ Shift: _____

Truck Number:_____ Electric:____ Internal Combustion:____

Hour Meter Start:_____ End:_____ Total Hours:_____

Check any defective item and explain in the notes section below:

| | | | |
|---|---|---|---|
| | Accelerator | | Hour Meter |
| | Alarms | | Hydraulic Controls |
| | Battery Connector | | Lights - Head and Tail |
| | Battery - Discharge Indicator | | Lights - Warning |
| | Belt | | Mast |
| | Brakes - Parking | | Oil Leaks |
| | Brakes - Service | | Oil Pressure |
| | Cables | | Overhead Guard |
| | Engine Oil Level | | Radiator Level |
| | Forks | | Safety Equipment |
| | Fuel | | Steering |
| | Gauges | | Tires |
| | Horn | | Unusual Noises |
| | Hoses | | Other _____ |

Notes:_____

_____

_____

_____

_____

_____

_____

_____

_____

Operator's Name:_____

Operator's Signature:_____

Supervisor's Name:_____

Supervisor's Signature:_____

Date: _____  Shift: _____

Truck Number:_____  Electric:____  Internal Combustion:____

Hour Meter Start:_____  End:_____  Total Hours:_____

Check any defective item and explain in the notes section below:

| | | | |
|---|---|---|---|
| | Accelerator | | Hour Meter |
| | Alarms | | Hydraulic Controls |
| | Battery Connector | | Lights - Head and Tail |
| | Battery - Discharge Indicator | | Lights - Warning |
| | Belt | | Mast |
| | Brakes - Parking | | Oil Leaks |
| | Brakes - Service | | Oil Pressure |
| | Cables | | Overhead Guard |
| | Engine Oil Level | | Radiator Level |
| | Forks | | Safety Equipment |
| | Fuel | | Steering |
| | Gauges | | Tires |
| | Horn | | Unusual Noises |
| | Hoses | | Other _____ |

Notes:_____

_____

_____

_____

_____

_____

_____

_____

_____

Operator's Name:_____

Operator's Signature:_____

Supervisor's Name:_____

Supervisor's Signature:_____

Date: _____ Shift: _____

Truck Number:_____ Electric:____ Internal Combustion:____

Hour Meter Start:_____ End:_____ Total Hours:_____

Check any defective item and explain in the notes section below:

| | | | |
|---|---|---|---|
| | Accelerator | | Hour Meter |
| | Alarms | | Hydraulic Controls |
| | Battery Connector | | Lights - Head and Tail |
| | Battery - Discharge Indicator | | Lights - Warning |
| | Belt | | Mast |
| | Brakes - Parking | | Oil Leaks |
| | Brakes - Service | | Oil Pressure |
| | Cables | | Overhead Guard |
| | Engine Oil Level | | Radiator Level |
| | Forks | | Safety Equipment |
| | Fuel | | Steering |
| | Gauges | | Tires |
| | Horn | | Unusual Noises |
| | Hoses | | Other _____ |

Notes:_____

_____

_____

_____

_____

_____

_____

_____

_____

_____

Operator's Name:_____

Operator's Signature:_____

Supervisor's Name:_____

Supervisor's Signature:_____

Date: _____ Shift: _____

Truck Number:_____ Electric:___ Internal Combustion:___

Hour Meter Start:_____ End:_____ Total Hours:_____

Check any defective item and explain in the notes section below:

| | | | |
|---|---|---|---|
| | Accelerator | | Hour Meter |
| | Alarms | | Hydraulic Controls |
| | Battery Connector | | Lights - Head and Tail |
| | Battery - Discharge Indicator | | Lights - Warning |
| | Belt | | Mast |
| | Brakes - Parking | | Oil Leaks |
| | Brakes - Service | | Oil Pressure |
| | Cables | | Overhead Guard |
| | Engine Oil Level | | Radiator Level |
| | Forks | | Safety Equipment |
| | Fuel | | Steering |
| | Gauges | | Tires |
| | Horn | | Unusual Noises |
| | Hoses | | Other _____ |

Notes:_____

_____

_____

_____

_____

_____

_____

_____

_____

Operator's Name:_____

Operator's Signature:_____

Supervisor's Name:_____

Supervisor's Signature:_____

Date: _____ Shift: _____

Truck Number:_____ Electric:____ Internal Combustion:____

Hour Meter Start:_____ End:_____ Total Hours:_____

Check any defective item and explain in the notes section below:

| | | | |
|---|---|---|---|
| | Accelerator | | Hour Meter |
| | Alarms | | Hydraulic Controls |
| | Battery Connector | | Lights - Head and Tail |
| | Battery - Discharge Indicator | | Lights - Warning |
| | Belt | | Mast |
| | Brakes - Parking | | Oil Leaks |
| | Brakes - Service | | Oil Pressure |
| | Cables | | Overhead Guard |
| | Engine Oil Level | | Radiator Level |
| | Forks | | Safety Equipment |
| | Fuel | | Steering |
| | Gauges | | Tires |
| | Horn | | Unusual Noises |
| | Hoses | | Other _____ |

Notes:_____

_____

_____

_____

_____

_____

_____

_____

_____

Operator's Name:_____

Operator's Signature:_____

Supervisor's Name:_____

Supervisor's Signature:_____

Date: _____ Shift: _____

Truck Number:_____ Electric:___ Internal Combustion:___

Hour Meter Start:_____ End:_____ Total Hours:_____

Check any defective item and explain in the notes section below:

| | | | |
|---|---|---|---|
| | Accelerator | | Hour Meter |
| | Alarms | | Hydraulic Controls |
| | Battery Connector | | Lights - Head and Tail |
| | Battery - Discharge Indicator | | Lights - Warning |
| | Belt | | Mast |
| | Brakes - Parking | | Oil Leaks |
| | Brakes - Service | | Oil Pressure |
| | Cables | | Overhead Guard |
| | Engine Oil Level | | Radiator Level |
| | Forks | | Safety Equipment |
| | Fuel | | Steering |
| | Gauges | | Tires |
| | Horn | | Unusual Noises |
| | Hoses | | Other _____ |

Notes:_____

_____

_____

_____

_____

_____

_____

_____

_____

_____

Operator's Name:_____

Operator's Signature:_____

Supervisor's Name:_____

Supervisor's Signature:_____

Date: _____ Shift: _____

Truck Number:_____ Electric:____ Internal Combustion:____

Hour Meter Start:_____ End:_____ Total Hours:_____

Check any defective item and explain in the notes section below:

| | | | |
|---|---|---|---|
| | Accelerator | | Hour Meter |
| | Alarms | | Hydraulic Controls |
| | Battery Connector | | Lights - Head and Tail |
| | Battery - Discharge Indicator | | Lights - Warning |
| | Belt | | Mast |
| | Brakes - Parking | | Oil Leaks |
| | Brakes - Service | | Oil Pressure |
| | Cables | | Overhead Guard |
| | Engine Oil Level | | Radiator Level |
| | Forks | | Safety Equipment |
| | Fuel | | Steering |
| | Gauges | | Tires |
| | Horn | | Unusual Noises |
| | Hoses | | Other _____ |

Notes:_____

_____

_____

_____

_____

_____

_____

_____

_____

Operator's Name:_____

Operator's Signature:_____

Supervisor's Name:_____

Supervisor's Signature:_____

Date: _____ Shift: _____

Truck Number:_____ Electric:___ Internal Combustion:___

Hour Meter Start:_____ End:_____ Total Hours:_____

Check any defective item and explain in the notes section below:

| | | | |
|---|---|---|---|
| | Accelerator | | Hour Meter |
| | Alarms | | Hydraulic Controls |
| | Battery Connector | | Lights - Head and Tail |
| | Battery - Discharge Indicator | | Lights - Warning |
| | Belt | | Mast |
| | Brakes - Parking | | Oil Leaks |
| | Brakes - Service | | Oil Pressure |
| | Cables | | Overhead Guard |
| | Engine Oil Level | | Radiator Level |
| | Forks | | Safety Equipment |
| | Fuel | | Steering |
| | Gauges | | Tires |
| | Horn | | Unusual Noises |
| | Hoses | | Other _____ |

Notes:_____

_____

_____

_____

_____

_____

_____

_____

_____

Operator's Name:_____

Operator's Signature:_____

Supervisor's Name:_____

Supervisor's Signature:_____

Date: _____ Shift: _____

Truck Number:_____ Electric:___ Internal Combustion:___

Hour Meter Start:_____ End:_____ Total Hours:_____

Check any defective item and explain in the notes section below:

| | | | |
|---|---|---|---|
| | Accelerator | | Hour Meter |
| | Alarms | | Hydraulic Controls |
| | Battery Connector | | Lights - Head and Tail |
| | Battery - Discharge Indicator | | Lights - Warning |
| | Belt | | Mast |
| | Brakes - Parking | | Oil Leaks |
| | Brakes - Service | | Oil Pressure |
| | Cables | | Overhead Guard |
| | Engine Oil Level | | Radiator Level |
| | Forks | | Safety Equipment |
| | Fuel | | Steering |
| | Gauges | | Tires |
| | Horn | | Unusual Noises |
| | Hoses | | Other _____ |

Notes:_____

_____

_____

_____

_____

_____

_____

_____

_____

Operator's Name:_____

Operator's Signature:_____

Supervisor's Name:_____

Supervisor's Signature:_____

Date: _____ Shift: _____

Truck Number:_____ Electric:___ Internal Combustion:___

Hour Meter Start:_____ End:_____ Total Hours:_____

Check any defective item and explain in the notes section below:

| | | | |
|---|---|---|---|
| | Accelerator | | Hour Meter |
| | Alarms | | Hydraulic Controls |
| | Battery Connector | | Lights - Head and Tail |
| | Battery - Discharge Indicator | | Lights - Warning |
| | Belt | | Mast |
| | Brakes - Parking | | Oil Leaks |
| | Brakes - Service | | Oil Pressure |
| | Cables | | Overhead Guard |
| | Engine Oil Level | | Radiator Level |
| | Forks | | Safety Equipment |
| | Fuel | | Steering |
| | Gauges | | Tires |
| | Horn | | Unusual Noises |
| | Hoses | | Other _____ |

Notes:_____

_____

_____

_____

_____

_____

_____

_____

_____

Operator's Name:_____

Operator's Signature:_____

Supervisor's Name:_____

Supervisor's Signature:_____

Date: _____  Shift: _____

Truck Number:_____  Electric:____  Internal Combustion:____

Hour Meter Start:_____  End:_____  Total Hours:_____

Check any defective item and explain in the notes section below:

| | | | |
|---|---|---|---|
| | Accelerator | | Hour Meter |
| | Alarms | | Hydraulic Controls |
| | Battery Connector | | Lights - Head and Tail |
| | Battery - Discharge Indicator | | Lights - Warning |
| | Belt | | Mast |
| | Brakes - Parking | | Oil Leaks |
| | Brakes - Service | | Oil Pressure |
| | Cables | | Overhead Guard |
| | Engine Oil Level | | Radiator Level |
| | Forks | | Safety Equipment |
| | Fuel | | Steering |
| | Gauges | | Tires |
| | Horn | | Unusual Noises |
| | Hoses | | Other _____ |

Notes:_____

_____

_____

_____

_____

_____

_____

_____

_____

Operator's Name:_____

Operator's Signature:_____

Supervisor's Name:_____

Supervisor's Signature:_____

Date: _____ Shift: _____

Truck Number:_____ Electric:___ Internal Combustion:___

Hour Meter Start:_____ End:_____ Total Hours:_____

Check any defective item and explain in the notes section below:

| | | | |
|---|---|---|---|
| | Accelerator | | Hour Meter |
| | Alarms | | Hydraulic Controls |
| | Battery Connector | | Lights - Head and Tail |
| | Battery - Discharge Indicator | | Lights - Warning |
| | Belt | | Mast |
| | Brakes - Parking | | Oil Leaks |
| | Brakes - Service | | Oil Pressure |
| | Cables | | Overhead Guard |
| | Engine Oil Level | | Radiator Level |
| | Forks | | Safety Equipment |
| | Fuel | | Steering |
| | Gauges | | Tires |
| | Horn | | Unusual Noises |
| | Hoses | | Other _____ |

Notes:_____

_____

_____

_____

_____

_____

_____

_____

_____

_____

Operator's Name:_____

Operator's Signature:_____

Supervisor's Name:_____

Supervisor's Signature:_____

Date: _____    Shift: _____

Truck Number:_____    Electric:____    Internal Combustion:____

Hour Meter Start:_____    End:_____    Total Hours:_____

Check any defective item and explain in the notes section below:

| | | | |
|---|---|---|---|
| | Accelerator | | Hour Meter |
| | Alarms | | Hydraulic Controls |
| | Battery Connector | | Lights - Head and Tail |
| | Battery - Discharge Indicator | | Lights - Warning |
| | Belt | | Mast |
| | Brakes - Parking | | Oil Leaks |
| | Brakes - Service | | Oil Pressure |
| | Cables | | Overhead Guard |
| | Engine Oil Level | | Radiator Level |
| | Forks | | Safety Equipment |
| | Fuel | | Steering |
| | Gauges | | Tires |
| | Horn | | Unusual Noises |
| | Hoses | | Other _____ |

Notes:_____

_____

_____

_____

_____

_____

_____

_____

_____

Operator's Name:_____

Operator's Signature:_____

Supervisor's Name:_____

Supervisor's Signature:_____

Date: _____ Shift: _____

Truck Number:_____ Electric:___ Internal Combustion:___

Hour Meter Start:_____ End:_____ Total Hours:_____

Check any defective item and explain in the notes section below:

| | | | |
|---|---|---|---|
| | Accelerator | | Hour Meter |
| | Alarms | | Hydraulic Controls |
| | Battery Connector | | Lights - Head and Tail |
| | Battery - Discharge Indicator | | Lights - Warning |
| | Belt | | Mast |
| | Brakes - Parking | | Oil Leaks |
| | Brakes - Service | | Oil Pressure |
| | Cables | | Overhead Guard |
| | Engine Oil Level | | Radiator Level |
| | Forks | | Safety Equipment |
| | Fuel | | Steering |
| | Gauges | | Tires |
| | Horn | | Unusual Noises |
| | Hoses | | Other _____ |

Notes:_____

_____

_____

_____

_____

_____

_____

_____

_____

_____

Operator's Name:_____

Operator's Signature:_____

Supervisor's Name:_____

Supervisor's Signature:_____

Date: _____ Shift: _____

Truck Number:_____ Electric:____ Internal Combustion:____

Hour Meter Start:_____ End:_____ Total Hours:_____

Check any defective item and explain in the notes section below:

| | | | |
|---|---|---|---|
| | Accelerator | | Hour Meter |
| | Alarms | | Hydraulic Controls |
| | Battery Connector | | Lights - Head and Tail |
| | Battery - Discharge Indicator | | Lights - Warning |
| | Belt | | Mast |
| | Brakes - Parking | | Oil Leaks |
| | Brakes - Service | | Oil Pressure |
| | Cables | | Overhead Guard |
| | Engine Oil Level | | Radiator Level |
| | Forks | | Safety Equipment |
| | Fuel | | Steering |
| | Gauges | | Tires |
| | Horn | | Unusual Noises |
| | Hoses | | Other _____ |

Notes:_____

_____

_____

_____

_____

_____

_____

_____

_____

Operator's Name:_____

Operator's Signature:_____

Supervisor's Name:_____

Supervisor's Signature:_____

Date: _____ Shift: _____

Truck Number:_____ Electric:____ Internal Combustion:____

Hour Meter Start:_____ End:_____ Total Hours:_____

Check any defective item and explain in the notes section below:

| | | | | |
|---|---|---|---|---|
| | Accelerator | | | Hour Meter |
| | Alarms | | | Hydraulic Controls |
| | Battery Connector | | | Lights - Head and Tail |
| | Battery - Discharge Indicator | | | Lights - Warning |
| | Belt | | | Mast |
| | Brakes - Parking | | | Oil Leaks |
| | Brakes - Service | | | Oil Pressure |
| | Cables | | | Overhead Guard |
| | Engine Oil Level | | | Radiator Level |
| | Forks | | | Safety Equipment |
| | Fuel | | | Steering |
| | Gauges | | | Tires |
| | Horn | | | Unusual Noises |
| | Hoses | | | Other _____ |

Notes:_____

_____

_____

_____

_____

_____

_____

_____

_____

Operator's Name:_____

Operator's Signature:_____

Supervisor's Name:_____

Supervisor's Signature:_____

Date: _____ Shift: _____

Truck Number: _____ Electric: ____ Internal Combustion: ____

Hour Meter Start: _____ End: _____ Total Hours: _____

Check any defective item and explain in the notes section below:

| | | | |
|---|---|---|---|
| | Accelerator | | Hour Meter |
| | Alarms | | Hydraulic Controls |
| | Battery Connector | | Lights - Head and Tail |
| | Battery - Discharge Indicator | | Lights - Warning |
| | Belt | | Mast |
| | Brakes - Parking | | Oil Leaks |
| | Brakes - Service | | Oil Pressure |
| | Cables | | Overhead Guard |
| | Engine Oil Level | | Radiator Level |
| | Forks | | Safety Equipment |
| | Fuel | | Steering |
| | Gauges | | Tires |
| | Horn | | Unusual Noises |
| | Hoses | | Other _____ |

Notes: _____
_____
_____
_____
_____
_____
_____
_____
_____

Operator's Name: _____

Operator's Signature: _____

Supervisor's Name: _____

Supervisor's Signature: _____

Date: _____  Shift: _____

Truck Number:_____  Electric:___  Internal Combustion:___

Hour Meter Start:_____ End:_____ Total Hours:_____

Check any defective item and explain in the notes section below:

| | | | |
|---|---|---|---|
| | Accelerator | | Hour Meter |
| | Alarms | | Hydraulic Controls |
| | Battery Connector | | Lights - Head and Tail |
| | Battery - Discharge Indicator | | Lights - Warning |
| | Belt | | Mast |
| | Brakes - Parking | | Oil Leaks |
| | Brakes - Service | | Oil Pressure |
| | Cables | | Overhead Guard |
| | Engine Oil Level | | Radiator Level |
| | Forks | | Safety Equipment |
| | Fuel | | Steering |
| | Gauges | | Tires |
| | Horn | | Unusual Noises |
| | Hoses | | Other _____ |

Notes:_____

_____

_____

_____

_____

_____

_____

_____

_____

_____

Operator's Name:_____

Operator's Signature:_____

Supervisor's Name:_____

Supervisor's Signature:_____

Date: _____  Shift: _____

Truck Number: _____  Electric: ____  Internal Combustion: ____

Hour Meter Start: _____  End: _____  Total Hours: _____

Check any defective item and explain in the notes section below:

| | | | |
|---|---|---|---|
| | Accelerator | | Hour Meter |
| | Alarms | | Hydraulic Controls |
| | Battery Connector | | Lights - Head and Tail |
| | Battery - Discharge Indicator | | Lights - Warning |
| | Belt | | Mast |
| | Brakes - Parking | | Oil Leaks |
| | Brakes - Service | | Oil Pressure |
| | Cables | | Overhead Guard |
| | Engine Oil Level | | Radiator Level |
| | Forks | | Safety Equipment |
| | Fuel | | Steering |
| | Gauges | | Tires |
| | Horn | | Unusual Noises |
| | Hoses | | Other _____ |

Notes:_____

_____

_____

_____

_____

_____

_____

_____

_____

Operator's Name:_____

Operator's Signature:_____

Supervisor's Name:_____

Supervisor's Signature:_____

Date: _____ Shift: _____

Truck Number:_____ Electric:___ Internal Combustion:___

Hour Meter Start:_____ End:_____ Total Hours:_____

Check any defective item and explain in the notes section below:

| | | | |
|---|---|---|---|
| | Accelerator | | Hour Meter |
| | Alarms | | Hydraulic Controls |
| | Battery Connector | | Lights - Head and Tail |
| | Battery - Discharge Indicator | | Lights - Warning |
| | Belt | | Mast |
| | Brakes - Parking | | Oil Leaks |
| | Brakes - Service | | Oil Pressure |
| | Cables | | Overhead Guard |
| | Engine Oil Level | | Radiator Level |
| | Forks | | Safety Equipment |
| | Fuel | | Steering |
| | Gauges | | Tires |
| | Horn | | Unusual Noises |
| | Hoses | | Other _____ |

Notes:_____

_____

_____

_____

_____

_____

_____

_____

_____

Operator's Name:_____

Operator's Signature:_____

Supervisor's Name:_____

Supervisor's Signature:_____

Date: _____ Shift: _____

Truck Number:_____ Electric:____ Internal Combustion:____

Hour Meter Start:_____ End:_____ Total Hours:_____

Check any defective item and explain in the notes section below:

| | | | |
|---|---|---|---|
| | Accelerator | | Hour Meter |
| | Alarms | | Hydraulic Controls |
| | Battery Connector | | Lights - Head and Tail |
| | Battery - Discharge Indicator | | Lights - Warning |
| | Belt | | Mast |
| | Brakes - Parking | | Oil Leaks |
| | Brakes - Service | | Oil Pressure |
| | Cables | | Overhead Guard |
| | Engine Oil Level | | Radiator Level |
| | Forks | | Safety Equipment |
| | Fuel | | Steering |
| | Gauges | | Tires |
| | Horn | | Unusual Noises |
| | Hoses | | Other _____ |

Notes:_____

_____

_____

_____

_____

_____

_____

_____

_____

Operator's Name:_____

Operator's Signature:_____

Supervisor's Name:_____

Supervisor's Signature:_____

Date: _____ Shift: _____

Truck Number:_____ Electric:____ Internal Combustion:____

Hour Meter Start:_____ End:_____ Total Hours:_____

Check any defective item and explain in the notes section below:

| | | | |
|---|---|---|---|
| | Accelerator | | Hour Meter |
| | Alarms | | Hydraulic Controls |
| | Battery Connector | | Lights - Head and Tail |
| | Battery - Discharge Indicator | | Lights - Warning |
| | Belt | | Mast |
| | Brakes - Parking | | Oil Leaks |
| | Brakes - Service | | Oil Pressure |
| | Cables | | Overhead Guard |
| | Engine Oil Level | | Radiator Level |
| | Forks | | Safety Equipment |
| | Fuel | | Steering |
| | Gauges | | Tires |
| | Horn | | Unusual Noises |
| | Hoses | | Other _____ |

Notes:_____

_____

_____

_____

_____

_____

_____

_____

_____

Operator's Name:_____

Operator's Signature:_____

Supervisor's Name:_____

Supervisor's Signature:_____

Date: _____ Shift: _____

Truck Number:_____ Electric:____ Internal Combustion:____

Hour Meter Start:_____ End:_____ Total Hours:_____

Check any defective item and explain in the notes section below:

| | | | |
|---|---|---|---|
| | Accelerator | | Hour Meter |
| | Alarms | | Hydraulic Controls |
| | Battery Connector | | Lights - Head and Tail |
| | Battery - Discharge Indicator | | Lights - Warning |
| | Belt | | Mast |
| | Brakes - Parking | | Oil Leaks |
| | Brakes - Service | | Oil Pressure |
| | Cables | | Overhead Guard |
| | Engine Oil Level | | Radiator Level |
| | Forks | | Safety Equipment |
| | Fuel | | Steering |
| | Gauges | | Tires |
| | Horn | | Unusual Noises |
| | Hoses | | Other _____ |

Notes:_____

_____

_____

_____

_____

_____

_____

_____

_____

Operator's Name:_____

Operator's Signature:_____

Supervisor's Name:_____

Supervisor's Signature:_____

Date: _____ Shift: _____

Truck Number: _____ Electric: ___ Internal Combustion: ___

Hour Meter Start: _____ End: _____ Total Hours: _____

Check any defective item and explain in the notes section below:

| | | | |
|---|---|---|---|
| | Accelerator | | Hour Meter |
| | Alarms | | Hydraulic Controls |
| | Battery Connector | | Lights - Head and Tail |
| | Battery - Discharge Indicator | | Lights - Warning |
| | Belt | | Mast |
| | Brakes - Parking | | Oil Leaks |
| | Brakes - Service | | Oil Pressure |
| | Cables | | Overhead Guard |
| | Engine Oil Level | | Radiator Level |
| | Forks | | Safety Equipment |
| | Fuel | | Steering |
| | Gauges | | Tires |
| | Horn | | Unusual Noises |
| | Hoses | | Other _____ |

Notes: _____

_____

_____

_____

_____

_____

_____

_____

_____

_____

Operator's Name: _____

Operator's Signature: _____

Supervisor's Name: _____

Supervisor's Signature: _____

Date: _____ Shift: _____

Truck Number:_____ Electric:____ Internal Combustion:____

Hour Meter Start:_____ End:_____ Total Hours:_____

Check any defective item and explain in the notes section below:

| | | | |
|---|---|---|---|
| | Accelerator | | Hour Meter |
| | Alarms | | Hydraulic Controls |
| | Battery Connector | | Lights - Head and Tail |
| | Battery - Discharge Indicator | | Lights - Warning |
| | Belt | | Mast |
| | Brakes - Parking | | Oil Leaks |
| | Brakes - Service | | Oil Pressure |
| | Cables | | Overhead Guard |
| | Engine Oil Level | | Radiator Level |
| | Forks | | Safety Equipment |
| | Fuel | | Steering |
| | Gauges | | Tires |
| | Horn | | Unusual Noises |
| | Hoses | | Other _____ |

Notes:_____
_____
_____
_____
_____
_____
_____
_____
_____

Operator's Name:_____

Operator's Signature:_____

Supervisor's Name:_____

Supervisor's Signature:_____

Date: _____ Shift: _____

Truck Number:_____ Electric:____ Internal Combustion:____

Hour Meter Start:_____ End:_____ Total Hours:_____

Check any defective item and explain in the notes section below:

| | | | |
|---|---|---|---|
| | Accelerator | | Hour Meter |
| | Alarms | | Hydraulic Controls |
| | Battery Connector | | Lights - Head and Tail |
| | Battery - Discharge Indicator | | Lights - Warning |
| | Belt | | Mast |
| | Brakes - Parking | | Oil Leaks |
| | Brakes - Service | | Oil Pressure |
| | Cables | | Overhead Guard |
| | Engine Oil Level | | Radiator Level |
| | Forks | | Safety Equipment |
| | Fuel | | Steering |
| | Gauges | | Tires |
| | Horn | | Unusual Noises |
| | Hoses | | Other _____ |

Notes:_____

_____

_____

_____

_____

_____

_____

_____

_____

_____

Operator's Name:_____

Operator's Signature:_____

Supervisor's Name:_____

Supervisor's Signature:_____

Date:_____ Shift:_____

Truck Number:_____ Electric:____ Internal Combustion:____

Hour Meter Start:_____ End:_____ Total Hours:_____

Check any defective item and explain in the notes section below:

| | | | |
|---|---|---|---|
| | Accelerator | | Hour Meter |
| | Alarms | | Hydraulic Controls |
| | Battery Connector | | Lights - Head and Tail |
| | Battery - Discharge Indicator | | Lights - Warning |
| | Belt | | Mast |
| | Brakes - Parking | | Oil Leaks |
| | Brakes - Service | | Oil Pressure |
| | Cables | | Overhead Guard |
| | Engine Oil Level | | Radiator Level |
| | Forks | | Safety Equipment |
| | Fuel | | Steering |
| | Gauges | | Tires |
| | Horn | | Unusual Noises |
| | Hoses | | Other _____ |

Notes:_____
_____
_____
_____
_____
_____
_____
_____
_____

Operator's Name:_____

Operator's Signature:_____

Supervisor's Name:_____

Supervisor's Signature:_____

Date: _____ Shift: _____

Truck Number: _____ Electric: ___ Internal Combustion: ___

Hour Meter Start: _____ End: _____ Total Hours: _____

Check any defective item and explain in the notes section below:

| | | | |
|---|---|---|---|
| | Accelerator | | Hour Meter |
| | Alarms | | Hydraulic Controls |
| | Battery Connector | | Lights - Head and Tail |
| | Battery - Discharge Indicator | | Lights - Warning |
| | Belt | | Mast |
| | Brakes - Parking | | Oil Leaks |
| | Brakes - Service | | Oil Pressure |
| | Cables | | Overhead Guard |
| | Engine Oil Level | | Radiator Level |
| | Forks | | Safety Equipment |
| | Fuel | | Steering |
| | Gauges | | Tires |
| | Horn | | Unusual Noises |
| | Hoses | | Other _____ |

Notes:_____

_____

_____

_____

_____

_____

_____

_____

_____

_____

Operator's Name:_____

Operator's Signature:_____

Supervisor's Name:_____

Supervisor's Signature:_____

Date: _____ Shift: _____

Truck Number:_____ Electric:___ Internal Combustion:___

Hour Meter Start:_____ End:_____ Total Hours:_____

Check any defective item and explain in the notes section below:

| | | | |
|---|---|---|---|
| | Accelerator | | Hour Meter |
| | Alarms | | Hydraulic Controls |
| | Battery Connector | | Lights - Head and Tail |
| | Battery - Discharge Indicator | | Lights - Warning |
| | Belt | | Mast |
| | Brakes - Parking | | Oil Leaks |
| | Brakes - Service | | Oil Pressure |
| | Cables | | Overhead Guard |
| | Engine Oil Level | | Radiator Level |
| | Forks | | Safety Equipment |
| | Fuel | | Steering |
| | Gauges | | Tires |
| | Horn | | Unusual Noises |
| | Hoses | | Other _____ |

Notes:_____
_____
_____
_____
_____
_____
_____
_____
_____

Operator's Name:_____

Operator's Signature:_____

Supervisor's Name:_____

Supervisor's Signature:_____

Date: _____ Shift: _____

Truck Number:_____ Electric:___ Internal Combustion:___

Hour Meter Start:_____ End:_____ Total Hours:_____

Check any defective item and explain in the notes section below:

| | | | |
|---|---|---|---|
| | Accelerator | | Hour Meter |
| | Alarms | | Hydraulic Controls |
| | Battery Connector | | Lights - Head and Tail |
| | Battery - Discharge Indicator | | Lights - Warning |
| | Belt | | Mast |
| | Brakes - Parking | | Oil Leaks |
| | Brakes - Service | | Oil Pressure |
| | Cables | | Overhead Guard |
| | Engine Oil Level | | Radiator Level |
| | Forks | | Safety Equipment |
| | Fuel | | Steering |
| | Gauges | | Tires |
| | Horn | | Unusual Noises |
| | Hoses | | Other _____ |

Notes:_____

_____

_____

_____

_____

_____

_____

_____

_____

Operator's Name:_____

Operator's Signature:_____

Supervisor's Name:_____

Supervisor's Signature:_____

Date: _____ Shift: _____

Truck Number:_____ Electric:____ Internal Combustion:____

Hour Meter Start:_____ End:_____ Total Hours:_____

Check any defective item and explain in the notes section below:

| | | | |
|---|---|---|---|
| | Accelerator | | Hour Meter |
| | Alarms | | Hydraulic Controls |
| | Battery Connector | | Lights - Head and Tail |
| | Battery - Discharge Indicator | | Lights - Warning |
| | Belt | | Mast |
| | Brakes - Parking | | Oil Leaks |
| | Brakes - Service | | Oil Pressure |
| | Cables | | Overhead Guard |
| | Engine Oil Level | | Radiator Level |
| | Forks | | Safety Equipment |
| | Fuel | | Steering |
| | Gauges | | Tires |
| | Horn | | Unusual Noises |
| | Hoses | | Other _____ |

Notes:_____
_____
_____
_____
_____
_____
_____
_____
_____

Operator's Name:_____

Operator's Signature:_____

Supervisor's Name:_____

Supervisor's Signature:_____

Date: _____ Shift: _____

Truck Number:_____ Electric:___ Internal Combustion:___

Hour Meter Start:_____ End:_____ Total Hours:_____

Check any defective item and explain in the notes section below:

| | | | |
|---|---|---|---|
| | Accelerator | | Hour Meter |
| | Alarms | | Hydraulic Controls |
| | Battery Connector | | Lights - Head and Tail |
| | Battery - Discharge Indicator | | Lights - Warning |
| | Belt | | Mast |
| | Brakes - Parking | | Oil Leaks |
| | Brakes - Service | | Oil Pressure |
| | Cables | | Overhead Guard |
| | Engine Oil Level | | Radiator Level |
| | Forks | | Safety Equipment |
| | Fuel | | Steering |
| | Gauges | | Tires |
| | Horn | | Unusual Noises |
| | Hoses | | Other _____ |

Notes:_____

_____

_____

_____

_____

_____

_____

_____

_____

Operator's Name:_____

Operator's Signature:_____

Supervisor's Name:_____

Supervisor's Signature:_____

Date: _____ Shift: _____

Truck Number:_____ Electric:____ Internal Combustion:____

Hour Meter Start:_____ End:_____ Total Hours:_____

Check any defective item and explain in the notes section below:

| | | | |
|---|---|---|---|
| | Accelerator | | Hour Meter |
| | Alarms | | Hydraulic Controls |
| | Battery Connector | | Lights - Head and Tail |
| | Battery - Discharge Indicator | | Lights - Warning |
| | Belt | | Mast |
| | Brakes - Parking | | Oil Leaks |
| | Brakes - Service | | Oil Pressure |
| | Cables | | Overhead Guard |
| | Engine Oil Level | | Radiator Level |
| | Forks | | Safety Equipment |
| | Fuel | | Steering |
| | Gauges | | Tires |
| | Horn | | Unusual Noises |
| | Hoses | | Other _____ |

Notes:_____
_____
_____
_____
_____
_____
_____
_____
_____

Operator's Name:_____

Operator's Signature:_____

Supervisor's Name:_____

Supervisor's Signature:_____

Date: _____ Shift: _____

Truck Number:_____ Electric:___ Internal Combustion:___

Hour Meter Start:_____ End:_____ Total Hours:_____

Check any defective item and explain in the notes section below:

| | | | |
|---|---|---|---|
| | Accelerator | | Hour Meter |
| | Alarms | | Hydraulic Controls |
| | Battery Connector | | Lights - Head and Tail |
| | Battery - Discharge Indicator | | Lights - Warning |
| | Belt | | Mast |
| | Brakes - Parking | | Oil Leaks |
| | Brakes - Service | | Oil Pressure |
| | Cables | | Overhead Guard |
| | Engine Oil Level | | Radiator Level |
| | Forks | | Safety Equipment |
| | Fuel | | Steering |
| | Gauges | | Tires |
| | Horn | | Unusual Noises |
| | Hoses | | Other _____ |

Notes:_____

_____

_____

_____

_____

_____

_____

_____

_____

Operator's Name:_____

Operator's Signature:_____

Supervisor's Name:_____

Supervisor's Signature:_____

Date: _____ Shift: _____

Truck Number: _____ Electric: ___ Internal Combustion: ___

Hour Meter Start: _____ End: _____ Total Hours: _____

Check any defective item and explain in the notes section below:

| | | | |
|---|---|---|---|
| | Accelerator | | Hour Meter |
| | Alarms | | Hydraulic Controls |
| | Battery Connector | | Lights - Head and Tail |
| | Battery - Discharge Indicator | | Lights - Warning |
| | Belt | | Mast |
| | Brakes - Parking | | Oil Leaks |
| | Brakes - Service | | Oil Pressure |
| | Cables | | Overhead Guard |
| | Engine Oil Level | | Radiator Level |
| | Forks | | Safety Equipment |
| | Fuel | | Steering |
| | Gauges | | Tires |
| | Horn | | Unusual Noises |
| | Hoses | | Other _____ |

Notes:_____

_____

_____

_____

_____

_____

_____

_____

_____

Operator's Name:_____

Operator's Signature:_____

Supervisor's Name:_____

Supervisor's Signature:_____

Date: _____  Shift: _____

Truck Number:_____  Electric:____  Internal Combustion:____

Hour Meter Start:_____  End:_____  Total Hours:_____

Check any defective item and explain in the notes section below:

| | | | | |
|---|---|---|---|---|
| | Accelerator | | | Hour Meter |
| | Alarms | | | Hydraulic Controls |
| | Battery Connector | | | Lights - Head and Tail |
| | Battery - Discharge Indicator | | | Lights - Warning |
| | Belt | | | Mast |
| | Brakes - Parking | | | Oil Leaks |
| | Brakes - Service | | | Oil Pressure |
| | Cables | | | Overhead Guard |
| | Engine Oil Level | | | Radiator Level |
| | Forks | | | Safety Equipment |
| | Fuel | | | Steering |
| | Gauges | | | Tires |
| | Horn | | | Unusual Noises |
| | Hoses | | | Other _____ |

Notes:_____

_____

_____

_____

_____

_____

_____

_____

_____

Operator's Name:_____

Operator's Signature:_____

Supervisor's Name:_____

Supervisor's Signature:_____

Date: _____ Shift: _____

Truck Number:_____ Electric:____ Internal Combustion:____

Hour Meter Start:_____ End:_____ Total Hours:_____

Check any defective item and explain in the notes section below:

| | | | |
|---|---|---|---|
| | Accelerator | | Hour Meter |
| | Alarms | | Hydraulic Controls |
| | Battery Connector | | Lights - Head and Tail |
| | Battery - Discharge Indicator | | Lights - Warning |
| | Belt | | Mast |
| | Brakes - Parking | | Oil Leaks |
| | Brakes - Service | | Oil Pressure |
| | Cables | | Overhead Guard |
| | Engine Oil Level | | Radiator Level |
| | Forks | | Safety Equipment |
| | Fuel | | Steering |
| | Gauges | | Tires |
| | Horn | | Unusual Noises |
| | Hoses | | Other _____ |

Notes:_____

_____

_____

_____

_____

_____

_____

_____

_____

_____

Operator's Name:_____

Operator's Signature:_____

Supervisor's Name:_____

Supervisor's Signature:_____

Date: _____  Shift: _____

Truck Number:_____  Electric:___  Internal Combustion:___

Hour Meter Start:_____ End:_____ Total Hours:_____

Check any defective item and explain in the notes section below:

| | | | |
|---|---|---|---|
| | Accelerator | | Hour Meter |
| | Alarms | | Hydraulic Controls |
| | Battery Connector | | Lights - Head and Tail |
| | Battery - Discharge Indicator | | Lights - Warning |
| | Belt | | Mast |
| | Brakes - Parking | | Oil Leaks |
| | Brakes - Service | | Oil Pressure |
| | Cables | | Overhead Guard |
| | Engine Oil Level | | Radiator Level |
| | Forks | | Safety Equipment |
| | Fuel | | Steering |
| | Gauges | | Tires |
| | Horn | | Unusual Noises |
| | Hoses | | Other _____ |

Notes:_____

_____

_____

_____

_____

_____

_____

_____

_____

Operator's Name:_____

Operator's Signature:_____

Supervisor's Name:_____

Supervisor's Signature:_____

Date: _____ Shift: _____

Truck Number:_____ Electric:___ Internal Combustion:___

Hour Meter Start:_____ End:_____ Total Hours:_____

Check any defective item and explain in the notes section below:

| | | | |
|---|---|---|---|
| | Accelerator | | Hour Meter |
| | Alarms | | Hydraulic Controls |
| | Battery Connector | | Lights - Head and Tail |
| | Battery - Discharge Indicator | | Lights - Warning |
| | Belt | | Mast |
| | Brakes - Parking | | Oil Leaks |
| | Brakes - Service | | Oil Pressure |
| | Cables | | Overhead Guard |
| | Engine Oil Level | | Radiator Level |
| | Forks | | Safety Equipment |
| | Fuel | | Steering |
| | Gauges | | Tires |
| | Horn | | Unusual Noises |
| | Hoses | | Other _____ |

Notes:_____
_____
_____
_____
_____
_____
_____
_____
_____

Operator's Name:_____

Operator's Signature:_____

Supervisor's Name:_____

Supervisor's Signature:_____

Date: _____     Shift: _____

Truck Number:_____     Electric:___  Internal Combustion:___

Hour Meter Start:_____  End:_____  Total Hours:_____

Check any defective item and explain in the notes section below:

| | | | |
|---|---|---|---|
| | Accelerator | | Hour Meter |
| | Alarms | | Hydraulic Controls |
| | Battery Connector | | Lights - Head and Tail |
| | Battery - Discharge Indicator | | Lights - Warning |
| | Belt | | Mast |
| | Brakes - Parking | | Oil Leaks |
| | Brakes - Service | | Oil Pressure |
| | Cables | | Overhead Guard |
| | Engine Oil Level | | Radiator Level |
| | Forks | | Safety Equipment |
| | Fuel | | Steering |
| | Gauges | | Tires |
| | Horn | | Unusual Noises |
| | Hoses | | Other _____ |

Notes:_____

_____

_____

_____

_____

_____

_____

_____

_____

Operator's Name:_____

Operator's Signature:_____

Supervisor's Name:_____

Supervisor's Signature:_____

Date: _____  Shift: _____

Truck Number:_____  Electric:____ Internal Combustion:____

Hour Meter Start:_____ End:_____ Total Hours:_____

Check any defective item and explain in the notes section below:

| | | | |
|---|---|---|---|
| | Accelerator | | Hour Meter |
| | Alarms | | Hydraulic Controls |
| | Battery Connector | | Lights - Head and Tail |
| | Battery - Discharge Indicator | | Lights - Warning |
| | Belt | | Mast |
| | Brakes - Parking | | Oil Leaks |
| | Brakes - Service | | Oil Pressure |
| | Cables | | Overhead Guard |
| | Engine Oil Level | | Radiator Level |
| | Forks | | Safety Equipment |
| | Fuel | | Steering |
| | Gauges | | Tires |
| | Horn | | Unusual Noises |
| | Hoses | | Other _____ |

Notes:_____

_____

_____

_____

_____

_____

_____

_____

_____

Operator's Name:_____

Operator's Signature:_____

Supervisor's Name:_____

Supervisor's Signature:_____

Date: _____ Shift: _____

Truck Number:_____ Electric:____ Internal Combustion:____

Hour Meter Start:_____ End:_____ Total Hours:_____

Check any defective item and explain in the notes section below:

| | | | |
|---|---|---|---|
| | Accelerator | | Hour Meter |
| | Alarms | | Hydraulic Controls |
| | Battery Connector | | Lights - Head and Tail |
| | Battery - Discharge Indicator | | Lights - Warning |
| | Belt | | Mast |
| | Brakes - Parking | | Oil Leaks |
| | Brakes - Service | | Oil Pressure |
| | Cables | | Overhead Guard |
| | Engine Oil Level | | Radiator Level |
| | Forks | | Safety Equipment |
| | Fuel | | Steering |
| | Gauges | | Tires |
| | Horn | | Unusual Noises |
| | Hoses | | Other _____ |

Notes:_____

_____

_____

_____

_____

_____

_____

_____

_____

Operator's Name:_____

Operator's Signature:_____

Supervisor's Name:_____

Supervisor's Signature:_____

Date: _____ Shift: _____

Truck Number:_____ Electric:____ Internal Combustion:____

Hour Meter Start:_____ End:_____ Total Hours:_____

Check any defective item and explain in the notes section below:

| | | | |
|---|---|---|---|
| | Accelerator | | Hour Meter |
| | Alarms | | Hydraulic Controls |
| | Battery Connector | | Lights - Head and Tail |
| | Battery - Discharge Indicator | | Lights - Warning |
| | Belt | | Mast |
| | Brakes - Parking | | Oil Leaks |
| | Brakes - Service | | Oil Pressure |
| | Cables | | Overhead Guard |
| | Engine Oil Level | | Radiator Level |
| | Forks | | Safety Equipment |
| | Fuel | | Steering |
| | Gauges | | Tires |
| | Horn | | Unusual Noises |
| | Hoses | | Other _____ |

Notes:_____

_____

_____

_____

_____

_____

_____

_____

_____

Operator's Name:_____

Operator's Signature:_____

Supervisor's Name:_____

Supervisor's Signature:_____

Date: _____ Shift: _____

Truck Number:_____ Electric:____ Internal Combustion:____

Hour Meter Start:_____ End:_____ Total Hours:_____

Check any defective item and explain in the notes section below:

| | | | |
|---|---|---|---|
| | Accelerator | | Hour Meter |
| | Alarms | | Hydraulic Controls |
| | Battery Connector | | Lights - Head and Tail |
| | Battery - Discharge Indicator | | Lights - Warning |
| | Belt | | Mast |
| | Brakes - Parking | | Oil Leaks |
| | Brakes - Service | | Oil Pressure |
| | Cables | | Overhead Guard |
| | Engine Oil Level | | Radiator Level |
| | Forks | | Safety Equipment |
| | Fuel | | Steering |
| | Gauges | | Tires |
| | Horn | | Unusual Noises |
| | Hoses | | Other _____ |

Notes:_____

_____

_____

_____

_____

_____

_____

_____

_____

Operator's Name:_____

Operator's Signature:_____

Supervisor's Name:_____

Supervisor's Signature:_____

Date: _____ Shift: _____

Truck Number:_____ Electric:___ Internal Combustion:___

Hour Meter Start:_____ End:_____ Total Hours:_____

Check any defective item and explain in the notes section below:

| | | | |
|---|---|---|---|
| | Accelerator | | Hour Meter |
| | Alarms | | Hydraulic Controls |
| | Battery Connector | | Lights - Head and Tail |
| | Battery - Discharge Indicator | | Lights - Warning |
| | Belt | | Mast |
| | Brakes - Parking | | Oil Leaks |
| | Brakes - Service | | Oil Pressure |
| | Cables | | Overhead Guard |
| | Engine Oil Level | | Radiator Level |
| | Forks | | Safety Equipment |
| | Fuel | | Steering |
| | Gauges | | Tires |
| | Horn | | Unusual Noises |
| | Hoses | | Other _____ |

Notes:_____

_____

_____

_____

_____

_____

_____

_____

_____

Operator's Name:_____

Operator's Signature:_____

Supervisor's Name:_____

Supervisor's Signature:_____

Date: _____   Shift: _____

Truck Number:_____   Electric:____   Internal Combustion:____

Hour Meter Start:_____ End:_____ Total Hours:_____

Check any defective item and explain in the notes section below:

| | | | |
|---|---|---|---|
| | Accelerator | | Hour Meter |
| | Alarms | | Hydraulic Controls |
| | Battery Connector | | Lights - Head and Tail |
| | Battery - Discharge Indicator | | Lights - Warning |
| | Belt | | Mast |
| | Brakes - Parking | | Oil Leaks |
| | Brakes - Service | | Oil Pressure |
| | Cables | | Overhead Guard |
| | Engine Oil Level | | Radiator Level |
| | Forks | | Safety Equipment |
| | Fuel | | Steering |
| | Gauges | | Tires |
| | Horn | | Unusual Noises |
| | Hoses | | Other _____ |

Notes:_____

_____

_____

_____

_____

_____

_____

_____

_____

_____

Operator's Name:_____

Operator's Signature:_____

Supervisor's Name:_____

Supervisor's Signature:_____

Date: _____ Shift: _____

Truck Number:_____ Electric:____ Internal Combustion:____

Hour Meter Start:_____ End:_____ Total Hours:_____

Check any defective item and explain in the notes section below:

| | | | |
|---|---|---|---|
| | Accelerator | | Hour Meter |
| | Alarms | | Hydraulic Controls |
| | Battery Connector | | Lights - Head and Tail |
| | Battery - Discharge Indicator | | Lights - Warning |
| | Belt | | Mast |
| | Brakes - Parking | | Oil Leaks |
| | Brakes - Service | | Oil Pressure |
| | Cables | | Overhead Guard |
| | Engine Oil Level | | Radiator Level |
| | Forks | | Safety Equipment |
| | Fuel | | Steering |
| | Gauges | | Tires |
| | Horn | | Unusual Noises |
| | Hoses | | Other _____ |

Notes:_____

_____

_____

_____

_____

_____

_____

_____

_____

Operator's Name:_____

Operator's Signature:_____

Supervisor's Name:_____

Supervisor's Signature:_____

Date: _____   Shift: _____

Truck Number:_____   Electric:___   Internal Combustion:___

Hour Meter Start:_____ End:_____ Total Hours:_____

Check any defective item and explain in the notes section below:

| | | | |
|---|---|---|---|
| | Accelerator | | Hour Meter |
| | Alarms | | Hydraulic Controls |
| | Battery Connector | | Lights - Head and Tail |
| | Battery - Discharge Indicator | | Lights - Warning |
| | Belt | | Mast |
| | Brakes - Parking | | Oil Leaks |
| | Brakes - Service | | Oil Pressure |
| | Cables | | Overhead Guard |
| | Engine Oil Level | | Radiator Level |
| | Forks | | Safety Equipment |
| | Fuel | | Steering |
| | Gauges | | Tires |
| | Horn | | Unusual Noises |
| | Hoses | | Other _____ |

Notes:_____

_____

_____

_____

_____

_____

_____

_____

_____

_____

Operator's Name:_____

Operator's Signature:_____

Supervisor's Name:_____

Supervisor's Signature:_____

Date: _____ Shift: _____

Truck Number:_____ Electric:____ Internal Combustion:____

Hour Meter Start:_____ End:_____ Total Hours:_____

Check any defective item and explain in the notes section below:

| | | | |
|---|---|---|---|
| | Accelerator | | Hour Meter |
| | Alarms | | Hydraulic Controls |
| | Battery Connector | | Lights - Head and Tail |
| | Battery - Discharge Indicator | | Lights - Warning |
| | Belt | | Mast |
| | Brakes - Parking | | Oil Leaks |
| | Brakes - Service | | Oil Pressure |
| | Cables | | Overhead Guard |
| | Engine Oil Level | | Radiator Level |
| | Forks | | Safety Equipment |
| | Fuel | | Steering |
| | Gauges | | Tires |
| | Horn | | Unusual Noises |
| | Hoses | | Other _____ |

Notes:_____
_____
_____
_____
_____
_____
_____
_____
_____

Operator's Name:_____

Operator's Signature:_____

Supervisor's Name:_____

Supervisor's Signature:_____

Date: _____ Shift: _____

Truck Number:_____ Electric:____ Internal Combustion:____

Hour Meter Start:_____ End:_____ Total Hours:_____

Check any defective item and explain in the notes section below:

| | | | | |
|---|---|---|---|---|
| | Accelerator | | | Hour Meter |
| | Alarms | | | Hydraulic Controls |
| | Battery Connector | | | Lights - Head and Tail |
| | Battery - Discharge Indicator | | | Lights - Warning |
| | Belt | | | Mast |
| | Brakes - Parking | | | Oil Leaks |
| | Brakes - Service | | | Oil Pressure |
| | Cables | | | Overhead Guard |
| | Engine Oil Level | | | Radiator Level |
| | Forks | | | Safety Equipment |
| | Fuel | | | Steering |
| | Gauges | | | Tires |
| | Horn | | | Unusual Noises |
| | Hoses | | | Other _____ |

Notes:_____

_____

_____

_____

_____

_____

_____

_____

_____

Operator's Name:_____

Operator's Signature:_____

Supervisor's Name:_____

Supervisor's Signature:_____

Date: _____  Shift: _____

Truck Number:_____  Electric:___  Internal Combustion:___

Hour Meter Start:_____ End:_____ Total Hours:_____

Check any defective item and explain in the notes section below:

| | | | |
|---|---|---|---|
| | Accelerator | | Hour Meter |
| | Alarms | | Hydraulic Controls |
| | Battery Connector | | Lights - Head and Tail |
| | Battery - Discharge Indicator | | Lights - Warning |
| | Belt | | Mast |
| | Brakes - Parking | | Oil Leaks |
| | Brakes - Service | | Oil Pressure |
| | Cables | | Overhead Guard |
| | Engine Oil Level | | Radiator Level |
| | Forks | | Safety Equipment |
| | Fuel | | Steering |
| | Gauges | | Tires |
| | Horn | | Unusual Noises |
| | Hoses | | Other _____ |

Notes:_____

_____

_____

_____

_____

_____

_____

_____

_____

Operator's Name:_____

Operator's Signature:_____

Supervisor's Name:_____

Supervisor's Signature:_____

Date: _____     Shift: _____

Truck Number:_____     Electric:____  Internal Combustion:____

Hour Meter Start:_____  End:_____  Total Hours:_____

Check any defective item and explain in the notes section below:

| | | | |
|---|---|---|---|
| | Accelerator | | Hour Meter |
| | Alarms | | Hydraulic Controls |
| | Battery Connector | | Lights - Head and Tail |
| | Battery - Discharge Indicator | | Lights - Warning |
| | Belt | | Mast |
| | Brakes - Parking | | Oil Leaks |
| | Brakes - Service | | Oil Pressure |
| | Cables | | Overhead Guard |
| | Engine Oil Level | | Radiator Level |
| | Forks | | Safety Equipment |
| | Fuel | | Steering |
| | Gauges | | Tires |
| | Horn | | Unusual Noises |
| | Hoses | | Other _____ |

Notes:_____
_____
_____
_____
_____
_____
_____
_____
_____
_____

Operator's Name:_____

Operator's Signature:_____

Supervisor's Name:_____

Supervisor's Signature:_____

Date: _____ Shift: _____

Truck Number:_____ Electric:____ Internal Combustion:____

Hour Meter Start:_____ End:_____ Total Hours:_____

Check any defective item and explain in the notes section below:

| | | | |
|---|---|---|---|
| | Accelerator | | Hour Meter |
| | Alarms | | Hydraulic Controls |
| | Battery Connector | | Lights - Head and Tail |
| | Battery - Discharge Indicator | | Lights - Warning |
| | Belt | | Mast |
| | Brakes - Parking | | Oil Leaks |
| | Brakes - Service | | Oil Pressure |
| | Cables | | Overhead Guard |
| | Engine Oil Level | | Radiator Level |
| | Forks | | Safety Equipment |
| | Fuel | | Steering |
| | Gauges | | Tires |
| | Horn | | Unusual Noises |
| | Hoses | | Other _____ |

Notes:_____
_____
_____
_____
_____
_____
_____
_____
_____

Operator's Name:_____

Operator's Signature:_____

Supervisor's Name:_____

Supervisor's Signature:_____

Date: _____ Shift: _____

Truck Number:_____ Electric:___ Internal Combustion:___

Hour Meter Start:_____ End:_____ Total Hours:_____

Check any defective item and explain in the notes section below:

| | | | |
|---|---|---|---|
| | Accelerator | | Hour Meter |
| | Alarms | | Hydraulic Controls |
| | Battery Connector | | Lights - Head and Tail |
| | Battery - Discharge Indicator | | Lights - Warning |
| | Belt | | Mast |
| | Brakes - Parking | | Oil Leaks |
| | Brakes - Service | | Oil Pressure |
| | Cables | | Overhead Guard |
| | Engine Oil Level | | Radiator Level |
| | Forks | | Safety Equipment |
| | Fuel | | Steering |
| | Gauges | | Tires |
| | Horn | | Unusual Noises |
| | Hoses | | Other _____ |

Notes:_____

_____

_____

_____

_____

_____

_____

_____

_____

Operator's Name:_____

Operator's Signature:_____

Supervisor's Name:_____

Supervisor's Signature:_____

Date: _____ Shift: _____

Truck Number:_____ Electric:____ Internal Combustion:____

Hour Meter Start:_____ End:_____ Total Hours:_____

Check any defective item and explain in the notes section below:

| | | | |
|---|---|---|---|
| | Accelerator | | Hour Meter |
| | Alarms | | Hydraulic Controls |
| | Battery Connector | | Lights - Head and Tail |
| | Battery - Discharge Indicator | | Lights - Warning |
| | Belt | | Mast |
| | Brakes - Parking | | Oil Leaks |
| | Brakes - Service | | Oil Pressure |
| | Cables | | Overhead Guard |
| | Engine Oil Level | | Radiator Level |
| | Forks | | Safety Equipment |
| | Fuel | | Steering |
| | Gauges | | Tires |
| | Horn | | Unusual Noises |
| | Hoses | | Other _____ |

Notes:_____

_____

_____

_____

_____

_____

_____

_____

_____

_____

Operator's Name:_____

Operator's Signature:_____

Supervisor's Name:_____

Supervisor's Signature:_____

Date: _____ Shift: _____

Truck Number:_____ Electric:____ Internal Combustion:____

Hour Meter Start:_____ End:_____ Total Hours:_____

Check any defective item and explain in the notes section below:

| | | | |
|---|---|---|---|
| | Accelerator | | Hour Meter |
| | Alarms | | Hydraulic Controls |
| | Battery Connector | | Lights - Head and Tail |
| | Battery - Discharge Indicator | | Lights - Warning |
| | Belt | | Mast |
| | Brakes - Parking | | Oil Leaks |
| | Brakes - Service | | Oil Pressure |
| | Cables | | Overhead Guard |
| | Engine Oil Level | | Radiator Level |
| | Forks | | Safety Equipment |
| | Fuel | | Steering |
| | Gauges | | Tires |
| | Horn | | Unusual Noises |
| | Hoses | | Other _____ |

Notes:_____

_____

_____

_____

_____

_____

_____

_____

_____

Operator's Name:_____

Operator's Signature:_____

Supervisor's Name:_____

Supervisor's Signature:_____

Date: _____ Shift: _____

Truck Number: _____ Electric: ___ Internal Combustion: ___

Hour Meter Start: _____ End: _____ Total Hours: _____

Check any defective item and explain in the notes section below:

| | | | |
|---|---|---|---|
| | Accelerator | | Hour Meter |
| | Alarms | | Hydraulic Controls |
| | Battery Connector | | Lights - Head and Tail |
| | Battery - Discharge Indicator | | Lights - Warning |
| | Belt | | Mast |
| | Brakes - Parking | | Oil Leaks |
| | Brakes - Service | | Oil Pressure |
| | Cables | | Overhead Guard |
| | Engine Oil Level | | Radiator Level |
| | Forks | | Safety Equipment |
| | Fuel | | Steering |
| | Gauges | | Tires |
| | Horn | | Unusual Noises |
| | Hoses | | Other _____ |

Notes: _____
_____
_____
_____
_____
_____
_____
_____
_____
_____

Operator's Name: _____

Operator's Signature: _____

Supervisor's Name: _____

Supervisor's Signature: _____

Date: _____ Shift: _____

Truck Number:_____ Electric:___ Internal Combustion:___

Hour Meter Start:_____ End:_____ Total Hours:_____

Check any defective item and explain in the notes section below:

| | | | |
|---|---|---|---|
| | Accelerator | | Hour Meter |
| | Alarms | | Hydraulic Controls |
| | Battery Connector | | Lights - Head and Tail |
| | Battery - Discharge Indicator | | Lights - Warning |
| | Belt | | Mast |
| | Brakes - Parking | | Oil Leaks |
| | Brakes - Service | | Oil Pressure |
| | Cables | | Overhead Guard |
| | Engine Oil Level | | Radiator Level |
| | Forks | | Safety Equipment |
| | Fuel | | Steering |
| | Gauges | | Tires |
| | Horn | | Unusual Noises |
| | Hoses | | Other _____ |

Notes:_____

_____

_____

_____

_____

_____

_____

_____

_____

_____

Operator's Name:_____

Operator's Signature:_____

Supervisor's Name:_____

Supervisor's Signature:_____

Date: _____ Shift: _____

Truck Number:_____ Electric:____ Internal Combustion:____

Hour Meter Start:_____ End:_____ Total Hours:_____

Check any defective item and explain in the notes section below:

| | | | |
|---|---|---|---|
| | Accelerator | | Hour Meter |
| | Alarms | | Hydraulic Controls |
| | Battery Connector | | Lights - Head and Tail |
| | Battery - Discharge Indicator | | Lights - Warning |
| | Belt | | Mast |
| | Brakes - Parking | | Oil Leaks |
| | Brakes - Service | | Oil Pressure |
| | Cables | | Overhead Guard |
| | Engine Oil Level | | Radiator Level |
| | Forks | | Safety Equipment |
| | Fuel | | Steering |
| | Gauges | | Tires |
| | Horn | | Unusual Noises |
| | Hoses | | Other _____ |

Notes:_____

_____

_____

_____

_____

_____

_____

_____

_____

_____

Operator's Name:_____

Operator's Signature:_____

Supervisor's Name:_____

Supervisor's Signature:_____

Date: _____ Shift: _____

Truck Number:_____ Electric:____ Internal Combustion:____

Hour Meter Start:_____ End:_____ Total Hours:_____

Check any defective item and explain in the notes section below:

| | | | |
|---|---|---|---|
| | Accelerator | | Hour Meter |
| | Alarms | | Hydraulic Controls |
| | Battery Connector | | Lights - Head and Tail |
| | Battery - Discharge Indicator | | Lights - Warning |
| | Belt | | Mast |
| | Brakes - Parking | | Oil Leaks |
| | Brakes - Service | | Oil Pressure |
| | Cables | | Overhead Guard |
| | Engine Oil Level | | Radiator Level |
| | Forks | | Safety Equipment |
| | Fuel | | Steering |
| | Gauges | | Tires |
| | Horn | | Unusual Noises |
| | Hoses | | Other _____ |

Notes:_____

_____

_____

_____

_____

_____

_____

_____

_____

Operator's Name:_____

Operator's Signature:_____

Supervisor's Name:_____

Supervisor's Signature:_____

Date: _____ Shift: _____

Truck Number:_____ Electric:____ Internal Combustion:____

Hour Meter Start:_____ End:_____ Total Hours:_____

Check any defective item and explain in the notes section below:

| | | | |
|---|---|---|---|
| | Accelerator | | Hour Meter |
| | Alarms | | Hydraulic Controls |
| | Battery Connector | | Lights - Head and Tail |
| | Battery - Discharge Indicator | | Lights - Warning |
| | Belt | | Mast |
| | Brakes - Parking | | Oil Leaks |
| | Brakes - Service | | Oil Pressure |
| | Cables | | Overhead Guard |
| | Engine Oil Level | | Radiator Level |
| | Forks | | Safety Equipment |
| | Fuel | | Steering |
| | Gauges | | Tires |
| | Horn | | Unusual Noises |
| | Hoses | | Other _____ |

Notes:_____

_____

_____

_____

_____

_____

_____

_____

_____

Operator's Name:_____

Operator's Signature:_____

Supervisor's Name:_____

Supervisor's Signature:_____

Date: _____ Shift: _____

Truck Number:_____ Electric:____ Internal Combustion:____

Hour Meter Start:_____ End:_____ Total Hours:_____

Check any defective item and explain in the notes section below:

| | | | |
|---|---|---|---|
| | Accelerator | | Hour Meter |
| | Alarms | | Hydraulic Controls |
| | Battery Connector | | Lights - Head and Tail |
| | Battery - Discharge Indicator | | Lights - Warning |
| | Belt | | Mast |
| | Brakes - Parking | | Oil Leaks |
| | Brakes - Service | | Oil Pressure |
| | Cables | | Overhead Guard |
| | Engine Oil Level | | Radiator Level |
| | Forks | | Safety Equipment |
| | Fuel | | Steering |
| | Gauges | | Tires |
| | Horn | | Unusual Noises |
| | Hoses | | Other _____ |

Notes:_____

_____

_____

_____

_____

_____

_____

_____

_____

Operator's Name:_____

Operator's Signature:_____

Supervisor's Name:_____

Supervisor's Signature:_____

Date: _____ Shift: _____

Truck Number:_____ Electric:___ Internal Combustion:___

Hour Meter Start:_____ End:_____ Total Hours:_____

Check any defective item and explain in the notes section below:

| | | | |
|---|---|---|---|
| | Accelerator | | Hour Meter |
| | Alarms | | Hydraulic Controls |
| | Battery Connector | | Lights - Head and Tail |
| | Battery - Discharge Indicator | | Lights - Warning |
| | Belt | | Mast |
| | Brakes - Parking | | Oil Leaks |
| | Brakes - Service | | Oil Pressure |
| | Cables | | Overhead Guard |
| | Engine Oil Level | | Radiator Level |
| | Forks | | Safety Equipment |
| | Fuel | | Steering |
| | Gauges | | Tires |
| | Horn | | Unusual Noises |
| | Hoses | | Other _____ |

Notes:_____

_____

_____

_____

_____

_____

_____

_____

_____

Operator's Name:_____

Operator's Signature:_____

Supervisor's Name:_____

Supervisor's Signature:_____

Date: _____   Shift: _____

Truck Number:_____   Electric:____   Internal Combustion:____

Hour Meter Start:_____   End:_____   Total Hours:_____

Check any defective item and explain in the notes section below:

| | | | |
|---|---|---|---|
| | Accelerator | | Hour Meter |
| | Alarms | | Hydraulic Controls |
| | Battery Connector | | Lights - Head and Tail |
| | Battery - Discharge Indicator | | Lights - Warning |
| | Belt | | Mast |
| | Brakes - Parking | | Oil Leaks |
| | Brakes - Service | | Oil Pressure |
| | Cables | | Overhead Guard |
| | Engine Oil Level | | Radiator Level |
| | Forks | | Safety Equipment |
| | Fuel | | Steering |
| | Gauges | | Tires |
| | Horn | | Unusual Noises |
| | Hoses | | Other _____ |

Notes:_____

_____

_____

_____

_____

_____

_____

_____

_____

Operator's Name:_____

Operator's Signature:_____

Supervisor's Name:_____

Supervisor's Signature:_____

Date: _____ Shift: _____

Truck Number:_____ Electric:____ Internal Combustion:____

Hour Meter Start:_____ End:_____ Total Hours:_____

Check any defective item and explain in the notes section below:

| | | | |
|---|---|---|---|
| | Accelerator | | Hour Meter |
| | Alarms | | Hydraulic Controls |
| | Battery Connector | | Lights - Head and Tail |
| | Battery - Discharge Indicator | | Lights - Warning |
| | Belt | | Mast |
| | Brakes - Parking | | Oil Leaks |
| | Brakes - Service | | Oil Pressure |
| | Cables | | Overhead Guard |
| | Engine Oil Level | | Radiator Level |
| | Forks | | Safety Equipment |
| | Fuel | | Steering |
| | Gauges | | Tires |
| | Horn | | Unusual Noises |
| | Hoses | | Other _____ |

Notes:_____

_____

_____

_____

_____

_____

_____

_____

_____

Operator's Name:_____

Operator's Signature:_____

Supervisor's Name:_____

Supervisor's Signature:_____

Date: _____  Shift: _____

Truck Number:_____  Electric:____  Internal Combustion:____

Hour Meter Start:_____  End:_____  Total Hours:_____

Check any defective item and explain in the notes section below:

| | Accelerator | | | Hour Meter |
|---|---|---|---|---|
| | Alarms | | | Hydraulic Controls |
| | Battery Connector | | | Lights - Head and Tail |
| | Battery - Discharge Indicator | | | Lights - Warning |
| | Belt | | | Mast |
| | Brakes - Parking | | | Oil Leaks |
| | Brakes - Service | | | Oil Pressure |
| | Cables | | | Overhead Guard |
| | Engine Oil Level | | | Radiator Level |
| | Forks | | | Safety Equipment |
| | Fuel | | | Steering |
| | Gauges | | | Tires |
| | Horn | | | Unusual Noises |
| | Hoses | | | Other _____ |

Notes:_____

_____

_____

_____

_____

_____

_____

_____

_____

Operator's Name:_____

Operator's Signature:_____

Supervisor's Name:_____

Supervisor's Signature:_____

Date: _____ Shift: _____

Truck Number:_____ Electric:____ Internal Combustion:____

Hour Meter Start:_____ End:_____ Total Hours:_____

Check any defective item and explain in the notes section below:

| | | | |
|---|---|---|---|
| | Accelerator | | Hour Meter |
| | Alarms | | Hydraulic Controls |
| | Battery Connector | | Lights - Head and Tail |
| | Battery - Discharge Indicator | | Lights - Warning |
| | Belt | | Mast |
| | Brakes - Parking | | Oil Leaks |
| | Brakes - Service | | Oil Pressure |
| | Cables | | Overhead Guard |
| | Engine Oil Level | | Radiator Level |
| | Forks | | Safety Equipment |
| | Fuel | | Steering |
| | Gauges | | Tires |
| | Horn | | Unusual Noises |
| | Hoses | | Other _____ |

Notes:_____
_____
_____
_____
_____
_____
_____
_____
_____

Operator's Name:_____

Operator's Signature:_____

Supervisor's Name:_____

Supervisor's Signature:_____

Date: _____ Shift: _____

Truck Number:_____ Electric:____ Internal Combustion:____

Hour Meter Start:_____ End:_____ Total Hours:_____

Check any defective item and explain in the notes section below:

| | | | |
|---|---|---|---|
| | Accelerator | | Hour Meter |
| | Alarms | | Hydraulic Controls |
| | Battery Connector | | Lights - Head and Tail |
| | Battery - Discharge Indicator | | Lights - Warning |
| | Belt | | Mast |
| | Brakes - Parking | | Oil Leaks |
| | Brakes - Service | | Oil Pressure |
| | Cables | | Overhead Guard |
| | Engine Oil Level | | Radiator Level |
| | Forks | | Safety Equipment |
| | Fuel | | Steering |
| | Gauges | | Tires |
| | Horn | | Unusual Noises |
| | Hoses | | Other _____ |

Notes:_____

_____

_____

_____

_____

_____

_____

_____

_____

Operator's Name:_____

Operator's Signature:_____

Supervisor's Name:_____

Supervisor's Signature:_____

Date: _____ Shift: _____

Truck Number:_____ Electric:____ Internal Combustion:____

Hour Meter Start:_____ End:_____ Total Hours:_____

Check any defective item and explain in the notes section below:

| | | | |
|---|---|---|---|
| | Accelerator | | Hour Meter |
| | Alarms | | Hydraulic Controls |
| | Battery Connector | | Lights - Head and Tail |
| | Battery - Discharge Indicator | | Lights - Warning |
| | Belt | | Mast |
| | Brakes - Parking | | Oil Leaks |
| | Brakes - Service | | Oil Pressure |
| | Cables | | Overhead Guard |
| | Engine Oil Level | | Radiator Level |
| | Forks | | Safety Equipment |
| | Fuel | | Steering |
| | Gauges | | Tires |
| | Horn | | Unusual Noises |
| | Hoses | | Other _____ |

Notes:_____

_____

_____

_____

_____

_____

_____

_____

_____

Operator's Name:_____

Operator's Signature:_____

Supervisor's Name:_____

Supervisor's Signature:_____

Date: _____ Shift: _____

Truck Number:_____ Electric:____ Internal Combustion:____

Hour Meter Start:_____ End:_____ Total Hours:_____

Check any defective item and explain in the notes section below:

| | | | |
|---|---|---|---|
| | Accelerator | | Hour Meter |
| | Alarms | | Hydraulic Controls |
| | Battery Connector | | Lights - Head and Tail |
| | Battery - Discharge Indicator | | Lights - Warning |
| | Belt | | Mast |
| | Brakes - Parking | | Oil Leaks |
| | Brakes - Service | | Oil Pressure |
| | Cables | | Overhead Guard |
| | Engine Oil Level | | Radiator Level |
| | Forks | | Safety Equipment |
| | Fuel | | Steering |
| | Gauges | | Tires |
| | Horn | | Unusual Noises |
| | Hoses | | Other _____ |

Notes:_____

_____

_____

_____

_____

_____

_____

_____

_____

Operator's Name:_____

Operator's Signature:_____

Supervisor's Name:_____

Supervisor's Signature:_____

Date: _____ Shift: _____

Truck Number:_____ Electric:___ Internal Combustion:___

Hour Meter Start:_____ End:_____ Total Hours:_____

Check any defective item and explain in the notes section below:

|  | | | |
|---|---|---|---|
|  | Accelerator |  | Hour Meter |
|  | Alarms |  | Hydraulic Controls |
|  | Battery Connector |  | Lights - Head and Tail |
|  | Battery - Discharge Indicator |  | Lights - Warning |
|  | Belt |  | Mast |
|  | Brakes - Parking |  | Oil Leaks |
|  | Brakes - Service |  | Oil Pressure |
|  | Cables |  | Overhead Guard |
|  | Engine Oil Level |  | Radiator Level |
|  | Forks |  | Safety Equipment |
|  | Fuel |  | Steering |
|  | Gauges |  | Tires |
|  | Horn |  | Unusual Noises |
|  | Hoses |  | Other _____ |

Notes:_____

_____

_____

_____

_____

_____

_____

_____

_____

Operator's Name:_____

Operator's Signature:_____

Supervisor's Name:_____

Supervisor's Signature:_____

Date: _____ Shift: _____

Truck Number:_____ Electric:____ Internal Combustion:____

Hour Meter Start:_____ End:_____ Total Hours:_____

Check any defective item and explain in the notes section below:

| | | | |
|---|---|---|---|
| | Accelerator | | Hour Meter |
| | Alarms | | Hydraulic Controls |
| | Battery Connector | | Lights - Head and Tail |
| | Battery - Discharge Indicator | | Lights - Warning |
| | Belt | | Mast |
| | Brakes - Parking | | Oil Leaks |
| | Brakes - Service | | Oil Pressure |
| | Cables | | Overhead Guard |
| | Engine Oil Level | | Radiator Level |
| | Forks | | Safety Equipment |
| | Fuel | | Steering |
| | Gauges | | Tires |
| | Horn | | Unusual Noises |
| | Hoses | | Other _____ |

Notes:_____

_____

_____

_____

_____

_____

_____

_____

_____

Operator's Name:_____

Operator's Signature:_____

Supervisor's Name:_____

Supervisor's Signature:_____

Date: _____ Shift: _____

Truck Number: _____ Electric: ____ Internal Combustion: ____

Hour Meter Start: _____ End: _____ Total Hours: _____

Check any defective item and explain in the notes section below:

| | | | |
|---|---|---|---|
| | Accelerator | | Hour Meter |
| | Alarms | | Hydraulic Controls |
| | Battery Connector | | Lights - Head and Tail |
| | Battery - Discharge Indicator | | Lights - Warning |
| | Belt | | Mast |
| | Brakes - Parking | | Oil Leaks |
| | Brakes - Service | | Oil Pressure |
| | Cables | | Overhead Guard |
| | Engine Oil Level | | Radiator Level |
| | Forks | | Safety Equipment |
| | Fuel | | Steering |
| | Gauges | | Tires |
| | Horn | | Unusual Noises |
| | Hoses | | Other _____ |

Notes: _____

_____

_____

_____

_____

_____

_____

_____

_____

Operator's Name: _____

Operator's Signature: _____

Supervisor's Name: _____

Supervisor's Signature: _____

Date: _____ Shift: _____

Truck Number:_____ Electric:___ Internal Combustion:___

Hour Meter Start:_____ End:_____ Total Hours:_____

Check any defective item and explain in the notes section below:

| | | | |
|---|---|---|---|
| | Accelerator | | Hour Meter |
| | Alarms | | Hydraulic Controls |
| | Battery Connector | | Lights - Head and Tail |
| | Battery - Discharge Indicator | | Lights - Warning |
| | Belt | | Mast |
| | Brakes - Parking | | Oil Leaks |
| | Brakes - Service | | Oil Pressure |
| | Cables | | Overhead Guard |
| | Engine Oil Level | | Radiator Level |
| | Forks | | Safety Equipment |
| | Fuel | | Steering |
| | Gauges | | Tires |
| | Horn | | Unusual Noises |
| | Hoses | | Other _____ |

Notes:_____

_____

_____

_____

_____

_____

_____

_____

_____

_____

Operator's Name:_____

Operator's Signature:_____

Supervisor's Name:_____

Supervisor's Signature:_____

Date: _____ Shift: _____

Truck Number:_____ Electric:___ Internal Combustion:___

Hour Meter Start:_____ End:_____ Total Hours:_____

Check any defective item and explain in the notes section below:

| | | | |
|---|---|---|---|
| | Accelerator | | Hour Meter |
| | Alarms | | Hydraulic Controls |
| | Battery Connector | | Lights - Head and Tail |
| | Battery - Discharge Indicator | | Lights - Warning |
| | Belt | | Mast |
| | Brakes - Parking | | Oil Leaks |
| | Brakes - Service | | Oil Pressure |
| | Cables | | Overhead Guard |
| | Engine Oil Level | | Radiator Level |
| | Forks | | Safety Equipment |
| | Fuel | | Steering |
| | Gauges | | Tires |
| | Horn | | Unusual Noises |
| | Hoses | | Other _____ |

Notes:_____

_____

_____

_____

_____

_____

_____

_____

_____

_____

Operator's Name:_____

Operator's Signature:_____

Supervisor's Name:_____

Supervisor's Signature:_____

Date: _____ Shift: _____

Truck Number:_____ Electric:___ Internal Combustion:___

Hour Meter Start:_____ End:_____ Total Hours:_____

Check any defective item and explain in the notes section below:

| | | | |
|---|---|---|---|
| | Accelerator | | Hour Meter |
| | Alarms | | Hydraulic Controls |
| | Battery Connector | | Lights - Head and Tail |
| | Battery - Discharge Indicator | | Lights - Warning |
| | Belt | | Mast |
| | Brakes - Parking | | Oil Leaks |
| | Brakes - Service | | Oil Pressure |
| | Cables | | Overhead Guard |
| | Engine Oil Level | | Radiator Level |
| | Forks | | Safety Equipment |
| | Fuel | | Steering |
| | Gauges | | Tires |
| | Horn | | Unusual Noises |
| | Hoses | | Other _____ |

Notes:_____

_____

_____

_____

_____

_____

_____

_____

_____

Operator's Name:_____

Operator's Signature:_____

Supervisor's Name:_____

Supervisor's Signature:_____

Date: _____ Shift: _____

Truck Number:_____ Electric:___ Internal Combustion:___

Hour Meter Start:_____ End:_____ Total Hours:_____

Check any defective item and explain in the notes section below:

| | | | |
|---|---|---|---|
| | Accelerator | | Hour Meter |
| | Alarms | | Hydraulic Controls |
| | Battery Connector | | Lights - Head and Tail |
| | Battery - Discharge Indicator | | Lights - Warning |
| | Belt | | Mast |
| | Brakes - Parking | | Oil Leaks |
| | Brakes - Service | | Oil Pressure |
| | Cables | | Overhead Guard |
| | Engine Oil Level | | Radiator Level |
| | Forks | | Safety Equipment |
| | Fuel | | Steering |
| | Gauges | | Tires |
| | Horn | | Unusual Noises |
| | Hoses | | Other _____ |

Notes:_____
_____
_____
_____
_____
_____
_____
_____
_____

Operator's Name:_____

Operator's Signature:_____

Supervisor's Name:_____

Supervisor's Signature:_____

Date: _____ Shift: _____

Truck Number:_____ Electric:____ Internal Combustion:____

Hour Meter Start:_____ End:_____ Total Hours:_____

Check any defective item and explain in the notes section below:

| | | | |
|---|---|---|---|
| | Accelerator | | Hour Meter |
| | Alarms | | Hydraulic Controls |
| | Battery Connector | | Lights - Head and Tail |
| | Battery - Discharge Indicator | | Lights - Warning |
| | Belt | | Mast |
| | Brakes - Parking | | Oil Leaks |
| | Brakes - Service | | Oil Pressure |
| | Cables | | Overhead Guard |
| | Engine Oil Level | | Radiator Level |
| | Forks | | Safety Equipment |
| | Fuel | | Steering |
| | Gauges | | Tires |
| | Horn | | Unusual Noises |
| | Hoses | | Other _____ |

Notes:_____

_____

_____

_____

_____

_____

_____

_____

_____

Operator's Name:_____

Operator's Signature:_____

Supervisor's Name:_____

Supervisor's Signature:_____

Date: _____ Shift: _____

Truck Number:_____ Electric:___ Internal Combustion:___

Hour Meter Start:_____ End:_____ Total Hours:_____

Check any defective item and explain in the notes section below:

| | | | |
|---|---|---|---|
| | Accelerator | | Hour Meter |
| | Alarms | | Hydraulic Controls |
| | Battery Connector | | Lights - Head and Tail |
| | Battery - Discharge Indicator | | Lights - Warning |
| | Belt | | Mast |
| | Brakes - Parking | | Oil Leaks |
| | Brakes - Service | | Oil Pressure |
| | Cables | | Overhead Guard |
| | Engine Oil Level | | Radiator Level |
| | Forks | | Safety Equipment |
| | Fuel | | Steering |
| | Gauges | | Tires |
| | Horn | | Unusual Noises |
| | Hoses | | Other _____ |

Notes:_____

_____

_____

_____

_____

_____

_____

_____

_____

Operator's Name:_____

Operator's Signature:_____

Supervisor's Name:_____

Supervisor's Signature:_____

Date: _____ Shift: _____

Truck Number:_____ Electric:___ Internal Combustion:___

Hour Meter Start:_____ End:_____ Total Hours:_____

Check any defective item and explain in the notes section below:

| | | | |
|---|---|---|---|
| | Accelerator | | Hour Meter |
| | Alarms | | Hydraulic Controls |
| | Battery Connector | | Lights - Head and Tail |
| | Battery - Discharge Indicator | | Lights - Warning |
| | Belt | | Mast |
| | Brakes - Parking | | Oil Leaks |
| | Brakes - Service | | Oil Pressure |
| | Cables | | Overhead Guard |
| | Engine Oil Level | | Radiator Level |
| | Forks | | Safety Equipment |
| | Fuel | | Steering |
| | Gauges | | Tires |
| | Horn | | Unusual Noises |
| | Hoses | | Other _____ |

Notes:_____

_____

_____

_____

_____

_____

_____

_____

_____

Operator's Name:_____

Operator's Signature:_____

Supervisor's Name:_____

Supervisor's Signature:_____

Date: _____ Shift: _____

Truck Number:_____ Electric:____ Internal Combustion:____

Hour Meter Start:_____ End:_____ Total Hours:_____

Check any defective item and explain in the notes section below:

| | | | |
|---|---|---|---|
| | Accelerator | | Hour Meter |
| | Alarms | | Hydraulic Controls |
| | Battery Connector | | Lights - Head and Tail |
| | Battery - Discharge Indicator | | Lights - Warning |
| | Belt | | Mast |
| | Brakes - Parking | | Oil Leaks |
| | Brakes - Service | | Oil Pressure |
| | Cables | | Overhead Guard |
| | Engine Oil Level | | Radiator Level |
| | Forks | | Safety Equipment |
| | Fuel | | Steering |
| | Gauges | | Tires |
| | Horn | | Unusual Noises |
| | Hoses | | Other _____ |

Notes:_____

_____

_____

_____

_____

_____

_____

_____

_____

Operator's Name:_____

Operator's Signature:_____

Supervisor's Name:_____

Supervisor's Signature:_____

Date: _____  Shift: _____

Truck Number:_____  Electric:___  Internal Combustion:___

Hour Meter Start:_____ End:_____ Total Hours:_____

Check any defective item and explain in the notes section below:

| | | | |
|---|---|---|---|
| | Accelerator | | Hour Meter |
| | Alarms | | Hydraulic Controls |
| | Battery Connector | | Lights - Head and Tail |
| | Battery - Discharge Indicator | | Lights - Warning |
| | Belt | | Mast |
| | Brakes - Parking | | Oil Leaks |
| | Brakes - Service | | Oil Pressure |
| | Cables | | Overhead Guard |
| | Engine Oil Level | | Radiator Level |
| | Forks | | Safety Equipment |
| | Fuel | | Steering |
| | Gauges | | Tires |
| | Horn | | Unusual Noises |
| | Hoses | | Other _____ |

Notes:_____

_____

_____

_____

_____

_____

_____

_____

_____

Operator's Name:_____

Operator's Signature:_____

Supervisor's Name:_____

Supervisor's Signature:_____

Date: _____ Shift: _____

Truck Number:_____ Electric:___ Internal Combustion:___

Hour Meter Start:_____ End:_____ Total Hours:_____

Check any defective item and explain in the notes section below:

| | | | |
|---|---|---|---|
| | Accelerator | | Hour Meter |
| | Alarms | | Hydraulic Controls |
| | Battery Connector | | Lights - Head and Tail |
| | Battery - Discharge Indicator | | Lights - Warning |
| | Belt | | Mast |
| | Brakes - Parking | | Oil Leaks |
| | Brakes - Service | | Oil Pressure |
| | Cables | | Overhead Guard |
| | Engine Oil Level | | Radiator Level |
| | Forks | | Safety Equipment |
| | Fuel | | Steering |
| | Gauges | | Tires |
| | Horn | | Unusual Noises |
| | Hoses | | Other _____ |

Notes:_____

_____

_____

_____

_____

_____

_____

_____

_____

Operator's Name:_____

Operator's Signature:_____

Supervisor's Name:_____

Supervisor's Signature:_____

Date: _____ Shift: _____

Truck Number:_____ Electric:____ Internal Combustion:____

Hour Meter Start:_____ End:_____ Total Hours:_____

Check any defective item and explain in the notes section below:

| | | | |
|---|---|---|---|
| | Accelerator | | Hour Meter |
| | Alarms | | Hydraulic Controls |
| | Battery Connector | | Lights - Head and Tail |
| | Battery - Discharge Indicator | | Lights - Warning |
| | Belt | | Mast |
| | Brakes - Parking | | Oil Leaks |
| | Brakes - Service | | Oil Pressure |
| | Cables | | Overhead Guard |
| | Engine Oil Level | | Radiator Level |
| | Forks | | Safety Equipment |
| | Fuel | | Steering |
| | Gauges | | Tires |
| | Horn | | Unusual Noises |
| | Hoses | | Other _____ |

Notes:_____

_____

_____

_____

_____

_____

_____

_____

_____

_____

Operator's Name:_____

Operator's Signature:_____

Supervisor's Name:_____

Supervisor's Signature:_____

Date: _____ Shift: _____

Truck Number:_____ Electric:____ Internal Combustion:____

Hour Meter Start:_____ End:_____ Total Hours:_____

Check any defective item and explain in the notes section below:

| | | | |
|---|---|---|---|
| | Accelerator | | Hour Meter |
| | Alarms | | Hydraulic Controls |
| | Battery Connector | | Lights - Head and Tail |
| | Battery - Discharge Indicator | | Lights - Warning |
| | Belt | | Mast |
| | Brakes - Parking | | Oil Leaks |
| | Brakes - Service | | Oil Pressure |
| | Cables | | Overhead Guard |
| | Engine Oil Level | | Radiator Level |
| | Forks | | Safety Equipment |
| | Fuel | | Steering |
| | Gauges | | Tires |
| | Horn | | Unusual Noises |
| | Hoses | | Other _____ |

Notes:_____
_____
_____
_____
_____
_____
_____
_____
_____

Operator's Name:_____

Operator's Signature:_____

Supervisor's Name:_____

Supervisor's Signature:_____

Date: _____ Shift: _____

Truck Number:_____ Electric:___ Internal Combustion:___

Hour Meter Start:_____ End:_____ Total Hours:_____

Check any defective item and explain in the notes section below:

| | | | |
|---|---|---|---|
| | Accelerator | | Hour Meter |
| | Alarms | | Hydraulic Controls |
| | Battery Connector | | Lights - Head and Tail |
| | Battery - Discharge Indicator | | Lights - Warning |
| | Belt | | Mast |
| | Brakes - Parking | | Oil Leaks |
| | Brakes - Service | | Oil Pressure |
| | Cables | | Overhead Guard |
| | Engine Oil Level | | Radiator Level |
| | Forks | | Safety Equipment |
| | Fuel | | Steering |
| | Gauges | | Tires |
| | Horn | | Unusual Noises |
| | Hoses | | Other _____ |

Notes:_____

_____

_____

_____

_____

_____

_____

_____

_____

Operator's Name:_____

Operator's Signature:_____

Supervisor's Name:_____

Supervisor's Signature:_____

Date: _____  Shift: _____

Truck Number:_____  Electric:___ Internal Combustion:___

Hour Meter Start:_____ End:_____ Total Hours:_____

Check any defective item and explain in the notes section below:

| | | | |
|---|---|---|---|
| | Accelerator | | Hour Meter |
| | Alarms | | Hydraulic Controls |
| | Battery Connector | | Lights - Head and Tail |
| | Battery - Discharge Indicator | | Lights - Warning |
| | Belt | | Mast |
| | Brakes - Parking | | Oil Leaks |
| | Brakes - Service | | Oil Pressure |
| | Cables | | Overhead Guard |
| | Engine Oil Level | | Radiator Level |
| | Forks | | Safety Equipment |
| | Fuel | | Steering |
| | Gauges | | Tires |
| | Horn | | Unusual Noises |
| | Hoses | | Other _____ |

Notes:_____

_____

_____

_____

_____

_____

_____

_____

_____

Operator's Name:_____

Operator's Signature:_____

Supervisor's Name:_____

Supervisor's Signature:_____

Date: _____ Shift: _____

Truck Number:_____ Electric:____ Internal Combustion:____

Hour Meter Start:_____ End:_____ Total Hours:_____

Check any defective item and explain in the notes section below:

| | | | |
|---|---|---|---|
| | Accelerator | | Hour Meter |
| | Alarms | | Hydraulic Controls |
| | Battery Connector | | Lights - Head and Tail |
| | Battery - Discharge Indicator | | Lights - Warning |
| | Belt | | Mast |
| | Brakes - Parking | | Oil Leaks |
| | Brakes - Service | | Oil Pressure |
| | Cables | | Overhead Guard |
| | Engine Oil Level | | Radiator Level |
| | Forks | | Safety Equipment |
| | Fuel | | Steering |
| | Gauges | | Tires |
| | Horn | | Unusual Noises |
| | Hoses | | Other _____ |

Notes:_____

_____

_____

_____

_____

_____

_____

_____

_____

Operator's Name:_____

Operator's Signature:_____

Supervisor's Name:_____

Supervisor's Signature:_____

Date: _____ Shift: _____

Truck Number: _____ Electric: ___ Internal Combustion: ___

Hour Meter Start: _____ End: _____ Total Hours: _____

Check any defective item and explain in the notes section below:

| | | | |
|---|---|---|---|
| | Accelerator | | Hour Meter |
| | Alarms | | Hydraulic Controls |
| | Battery Connector | | Lights - Head and Tail |
| | Battery - Discharge Indicator | | Lights - Warning |
| | Belt | | Mast |
| | Brakes - Parking | | Oil Leaks |
| | Brakes - Service | | Oil Pressure |
| | Cables | | Overhead Guard |
| | Engine Oil Level | | Radiator Level |
| | Forks | | Safety Equipment |
| | Fuel | | Steering |
| | Gauges | | Tires |
| | Horn | | Unusual Noises |
| | Hoses | | Other _____ |

Notes: _____

_____

_____

_____

_____

_____

_____

_____

_____

Operator's Name: _____

Operator's Signature: _____

Supervisor's Name: _____

Supervisor's Signature: _____

Date: _____ Shift: _____

Truck Number:_____ Electric:____ Internal Combustion:____

Hour Meter Start:_____ End:_____ Total Hours:_____

Check any defective item and explain in the notes section below:

| | | | |
|---|---|---|---|
| | Accelerator | | Hour Meter |
| | Alarms | | Hydraulic Controls |
| | Battery Connector | | Lights - Head and Tail |
| | Battery - Discharge Indicator | | Lights - Warning |
| | Belt | | Mast |
| | Brakes - Parking | | Oil Leaks |
| | Brakes - Service | | Oil Pressure |
| | Cables | | Overhead Guard |
| | Engine Oil Level | | Radiator Level |
| | Forks | | Safety Equipment |
| | Fuel | | Steering |
| | Gauges | | Tires |
| | Horn | | Unusual Noises |
| | Hoses | | Other _____ |

Notes:_____

_____

_____

_____

_____

_____

_____

_____

_____

_____

Operator's Name:_____

Operator's Signature:_____

Supervisor's Name:_____

Supervisor's Signature:_____

Date: _____ Shift: _____

Truck Number:_____ Electric:____ Internal Combustion:____

Hour Meter Start:_____ End:_____ Total Hours:_____

Check any defective item and explain in the notes section below:

| | | | |
|---|---|---|---|
| | Accelerator | | Hour Meter |
| | Alarms | | Hydraulic Controls |
| | Battery Connector | | Lights - Head and Tail |
| | Battery - Discharge Indicator | | Lights - Warning |
| | Belt | | Mast |
| | Brakes - Parking | | Oil Leaks |
| | Brakes - Service | | Oil Pressure |
| | Cables | | Overhead Guard |
| | Engine Oil Level | | Radiator Level |
| | Forks | | Safety Equipment |
| | Fuel | | Steering |
| | Gauges | | Tires |
| | Horn | | Unusual Noises |
| | Hoses | | Other _____ |

Notes:_____
_____
_____
_____
_____
_____
_____
_____
_____
_____

Operator's Name:_____

Operator's Signature:_____

Supervisor's Name:_____

Supervisor's Signature:_____

Date: _____ Shift: _____

Truck Number:_____ Electric:____ Internal Combustion:____

Hour Meter Start:_____ End:_____ Total Hours:_____

Check any defective item and explain in the notes section below:

| | | | |
|---|---|---|---|
| | Accelerator | | Hour Meter |
| | Alarms | | Hydraulic Controls |
| | Battery Connector | | Lights - Head and Tail |
| | Battery - Discharge Indicator | | Lights - Warning |
| | Belt | | Mast |
| | Brakes - Parking | | Oil Leaks |
| | Brakes - Service | | Oil Pressure |
| | Cables | | Overhead Guard |
| | Engine Oil Level | | Radiator Level |
| | Forks | | Safety Equipment |
| | Fuel | | Steering |
| | Gauges | | Tires |
| | Horn | | Unusual Noises |
| | Hoses | | Other _____ |

Notes:_____

_____

_____

_____

_____

_____

_____

_____

_____

Operator's Name:_____

Operator's Signature:_____

Supervisor's Name:_____

Supervisor's Signature:_____

Date: _____    Shift: _____

Truck Number:_____    Electric:____    Internal Combustion:____

Hour Meter Start:_____    End:_____    Total Hours:_____

Check any defective item and explain in the notes section below:

| | | | |
|---|---|---|---|
| | Accelerator | | Hour Meter |
| | Alarms | | Hydraulic Controls |
| | Battery Connector | | Lights - Head and Tail |
| | Battery - Discharge Indicator | | Lights - Warning |
| | Belt | | Mast |
| | Brakes - Parking | | Oil Leaks |
| | Brakes - Service | | Oil Pressure |
| | Cables | | Overhead Guard |
| | Engine Oil Level | | Radiator Level |
| | Forks | | Safety Equipment |
| | Fuel | | Steering |
| | Gauges | | Tires |
| | Horn | | Unusual Noises |
| | Hoses | | Other _____ |

Notes:_____

_____

_____

_____

_____

_____

_____

_____

_____

Operator's Name:_____

Operator's Signature:_____

Supervisor's Name:_____

Supervisor's Signature:_____

Date: _____   Shift: _____

Truck Number:_____   Electric:___   Internal Combustion:___

Hour Meter Start:_____ End:_____ Total Hours:_____

Check any defective item and explain in the notes section below:

| | | | |
|---|---|---|---|
| | Accelerator | | Hour Meter |
| | Alarms | | Hydraulic Controls |
| | Battery Connector | | Lights - Head and Tail |
| | Battery - Discharge Indicator | | Lights - Warning |
| | Belt | | Mast |
| | Brakes - Parking | | Oil Leaks |
| | Brakes - Service | | Oil Pressure |
| | Cables | | Overhead Guard |
| | Engine Oil Level | | Radiator Level |
| | Forks | | Safety Equipment |
| | Fuel | | Steering |
| | Gauges | | Tires |
| | Horn | | Unusual Noises |
| | Hoses | | Other _____ |

Notes:_____

_____

_____

_____

_____

_____

_____

_____

_____

Operator's Name:_____

Operator's Signature:_____

Supervisor's Name:_____

Supervisor's Signature:_____

Date: _____ Shift: _____

Truck Number:_____ Electric:____ Internal Combustion:____

Hour Meter Start:_____ End:_____ Total Hours:_____

Check any defective item and explain in the notes section below:

| | | | |
|---|---|---|---|
| | Accelerator | | Hour Meter |
| | Alarms | | Hydraulic Controls |
| | Battery Connector | | Lights - Head and Tail |
| | Battery - Discharge Indicator | | Lights - Warning |
| | Belt | | Mast |
| | Brakes - Parking | | Oil Leaks |
| | Brakes - Service | | Oil Pressure |
| | Cables | | Overhead Guard |
| | Engine Oil Level | | Radiator Level |
| | Forks | | Safety Equipment |
| | Fuel | | Steering |
| | Gauges | | Tires |
| | Horn | | Unusual Noises |
| | Hoses | | Other _____ |

Notes:_____

_____

_____

_____

_____

_____

_____

_____

_____

Operator's Name:_____

Operator's Signature:_____

Supervisor's Name:_____

Supervisor's Signature:_____

Date: _____     Shift: _____

Truck Number:_____  Electric:___  Internal Combustion:___

Hour Meter Start:_____  End:_____  Total Hours:_____

Check any defective item and explain in the notes section below:

| | | | |
|---|---|---|---|
| | Accelerator | | Hour Meter |
| | Alarms | | Hydraulic Controls |
| | Battery Connector | | Lights - Head and Tail |
| | Battery - Discharge Indicator | | Lights - Warning |
| | Belt | | Mast |
| | Brakes - Parking | | Oil Leaks |
| | Brakes - Service | | Oil Pressure |
| | Cables | | Overhead Guard |
| | Engine Oil Level | | Radiator Level |
| | Forks | | Safety Equipment |
| | Fuel | | Steering |
| | Gauges | | Tires |
| | Horn | | Unusual Noises |
| | Hoses | | Other _____ |

Notes:_____

_____

_____

_____

_____

_____

_____

_____

_____

Operator's Name:_____

Operator's Signature:_____

Supervisor's Name:_____

Supervisor's Signature:_____

Date: _____  Shift: _____

Truck Number: _____  Electric: ___  Internal Combustion: ___

Hour Meter Start: _____  End: _____  Total Hours: _____

Check any defective item and explain in the notes section below:

| | | | |
|---|---|---|---|
| | Accelerator | | Hour Meter |
| | Alarms | | Hydraulic Controls |
| | Battery Connector | | Lights - Head and Tail |
| | Battery - Discharge Indicator | | Lights - Warning |
| | Belt | | Mast |
| | Brakes - Parking | | Oil Leaks |
| | Brakes - Service | | Oil Pressure |
| | Cables | | Overhead Guard |
| | Engine Oil Level | | Radiator Level |
| | Forks | | Safety Equipment |
| | Fuel | | Steering |
| | Gauges | | Tires |
| | Horn | | Unusual Noises |
| | Hoses | | Other _____ |

Notes: _____

_____

_____

_____

_____

_____

_____

_____

_____

Operator's Name: _____

Operator's Signature: _____

Supervisor's Name: _____

Supervisor's Signature: _____

Date:_____ Shift:_____

Truck Number:_____ Electric:___ Internal Combustion:___

Hour Meter Start:_____ End:_____ Total Hours:_____

Check any defective item and explain in the notes section below:

| | | | |
|---|---|---|---|
| | Accelerator | | Hour Meter |
| | Alarms | | Hydraulic Controls |
| | Battery Connector | | Lights - Head and Tail |
| | Battery - Discharge Indicator | | Lights - Warning |
| | Belt | | Mast |
| | Brakes - Parking | | Oil Leaks |
| | Brakes - Service | | Oil Pressure |
| | Cables | | Overhead Guard |
| | Engine Oil Level | | Radiator Level |
| | Forks | | Safety Equipment |
| | Fuel | | Steering |
| | Gauges | | Tires |
| | Horn | | Unusual Noises |
| | Hoses | | Other _____ |

Notes:_____

_____

_____

_____

_____

_____

_____

_____

_____

Operator's Name:_____

Operator's Signature:_____

Supervisor's Name:_____

Supervisor's Signature:_____

Date: _____ Shift: _____

Truck Number:_____ Electric:____ Internal Combustion:____

Hour Meter Start:_____ End:_____ Total Hours:_____

Check any defective item and explain in the notes section below:

| | | | |
|---|---|---|---|
| | Accelerator | | Hour Meter |
| | Alarms | | Hydraulic Controls |
| | Battery Connector | | Lights - Head and Tail |
| | Battery - Discharge Indicator | | Lights - Warning |
| | Belt | | Mast |
| | Brakes - Parking | | Oil Leaks |
| | Brakes - Service | | Oil Pressure |
| | Cables | | Overhead Guard |
| | Engine Oil Level | | Radiator Level |
| | Forks | | Safety Equipment |
| | Fuel | | Steering |
| | Gauges | | Tires |
| | Horn | | Unusual Noises |
| | Hoses | | Other _____ |

Notes:_____

_____

_____

_____

_____

_____

_____

_____

_____

Operator's Name:_____

Operator's Signature:_____

Supervisor's Name:_____

Supervisor's Signature:_____

Date: _____ Shift: _____

Truck Number:_____ Electric:____ Internal Combustion:____

Hour Meter Start:_____ End:_____ Total Hours:_____

Check any defective item and explain in the notes section below:

| | | | |
|---|---|---|---|
| | Accelerator | | Hour Meter |
| | Alarms | | Hydraulic Controls |
| | Battery Connector | | Lights - Head and Tail |
| | Battery - Discharge Indicator | | Lights - Warning |
| | Belt | | Mast |
| | Brakes - Parking | | Oil Leaks |
| | Brakes - Service | | Oil Pressure |
| | Cables | | Overhead Guard |
| | Engine Oil Level | | Radiator Level |
| | Forks | | Safety Equipment |
| | Fuel | | Steering |
| | Gauges | | Tires |
| | Horn | | Unusual Noises |
| | Hoses | | Other _____ |

Notes:_____

_____

_____

_____

_____

_____

_____

_____

_____

_____

Operator's Name:_____

Operator's Signature:_____

Supervisor's Name:_____

Supervisor's Signature:_____

Date: _____ Shift: _____

Truck Number:_____ Electric:____ Internal Combustion:____

Hour Meter Start:_____ End:_____ Total Hours:_____

Check any defective item and explain in the notes section below:

| | | | |
|---|---|---|---|
| | Accelerator | | Hour Meter |
| | Alarms | | Hydraulic Controls |
| | Battery Connector | | Lights - Head and Tail |
| | Battery - Discharge Indicator | | Lights - Warning |
| | Belt | | Mast |
| | Brakes - Parking | | Oil Leaks |
| | Brakes - Service | | Oil Pressure |
| | Cables | | Overhead Guard |
| | Engine Oil Level | | Radiator Level |
| | Forks | | Safety Equipment |
| | Fuel | | Steering |
| | Gauges | | Tires |
| | Horn | | Unusual Noises |
| | Hoses | | Other _____ |

Notes:_____

_____

_____

_____

_____

_____

_____

_____

_____

Operator's Name:_____

Operator's Signature:_____

Supervisor's Name:_____

Supervisor's Signature:_____

Date: _____ Shift: _____

Truck Number:_____ Electric:____ Internal Combustion:____

Hour Meter Start:_____ End:_____ Total Hours:_____

Check any defective item and explain in the notes section below:

| | | | |
|---|---|---|---|
| | Accelerator | | Hour Meter |
| | Alarms | | Hydraulic Controls |
| | Battery Connector | | Lights - Head and Tail |
| | Battery - Discharge Indicator | | Lights - Warning |
| | Belt | | Mast |
| | Brakes - Parking | | Oil Leaks |
| | Brakes - Service | | Oil Pressure |
| | Cables | | Overhead Guard |
| | Engine Oil Level | | Radiator Level |
| | Forks | | Safety Equipment |
| | Fuel | | Steering |
| | Gauges | | Tires |
| | Horn | | Unusual Noises |
| | Hoses | | Other _____ |

Notes:_____

_____

_____

_____

_____

_____

_____

_____

_____

Operator's Name:_____

Operator's Signature:_____

Supervisor's Name:_____

Supervisor's Signature:_____

Date: _____  Shift: _____

Truck Number: _____  Electric: ____  Internal Combustion: ____

Hour Meter Start: _____  End: _____  Total Hours: _____

Check any defective item and explain in the notes section below:

|  |  |  |  |
|---|---|---|---|
|  | Accelerator |  | Hour Meter |
|  | Alarms |  | Hydraulic Controls |
|  | Battery Connector |  | Lights - Head and Tail |
|  | Battery - Discharge Indicator |  | Lights - Warning |
|  | Belt |  | Mast |
|  | Brakes - Parking |  | Oil Leaks |
|  | Brakes - Service |  | Oil Pressure |
|  | Cables |  | Overhead Guard |
|  | Engine Oil Level |  | Radiator Level |
|  | Forks |  | Safety Equipment |
|  | Fuel |  | Steering |
|  | Gauges |  | Tires |
|  | Horn |  | Unusual Noises |
|  | Hoses |  | Other _____ |

Notes: _____
_____
_____
_____
_____
_____
_____
_____
_____

Operator's Name: _____

Operator's Signature: _____

Supervisor's Name: _____

Supervisor's Signature: _____

Date: _____ Shift: _____

Truck Number: _____ Electric: ____ Internal Combustion: ___

Hour Meter Start: _____ End: _____ Total Hours: _____

Check any defective item and explain in the notes section below:

| | | | |
|---|---|---|---|
| | Accelerator | | Hour Meter |
| | Alarms | | Hydraulic Controls |
| | Battery Connector | | Lights - Head and Tail |
| | Battery - Discharge Indicator | | Lights - Warning |
| | Belt | | Mast |
| | Brakes - Parking | | Oil Leaks |
| | Brakes - Service | | Oil Pressure |
| | Cables | | Overhead Guard |
| | Engine Oil Level | | Radiator Level |
| | Forks | | Safety Equipment |
| | Fuel | | Steering |
| | Gauges | | Tires |
| | Horn | | Unusual Noises |
| | Hoses | | Other _____ |

Notes: _____
_____
_____
_____
_____
_____
_____
_____
_____

Operator's Name: _____

Operator's Signature: _____

Supervisor's Name: _____

Supervisor's Signature: _____

Date: _____ Shift: _____

Truck Number: _____ Electric: ____ Internal Combustion: ____

Hour Meter Start: _____ End: _____ Total Hours: _____

Check any defective item and explain in the notes section below:

| | | | |
|---|---|---|---|
| | Accelerator | | Hour Meter |
| | Alarms | | Hydraulic Controls |
| | Battery Connector | | Lights - Head and Tail |
| | Battery - Discharge Indicator | | Lights - Warning |
| | Belt | | Mast |
| | Brakes - Parking | | Oil Leaks |
| | Brakes - Service | | Oil Pressure |
| | Cables | | Overhead Guard |
| | Engine Oil Level | | Radiator Level |
| | Forks | | Safety Equipment |
| | Fuel | | Steering |
| | Gauges | | Tires |
| | Horn | | Unusual Noises |
| | Hoses | | Other _____ |

Notes: _____
_____
_____
_____
_____
_____
_____
_____
_____
_____

Operator's Name: _____

Operator's Signature: _____

Supervisor's Name: _____

Supervisor's Signature: _____

Date: _____ Shift: _____

Truck Number:_____ Electric:___ Internal Combustion:___

Hour Meter Start:_____ End:_____ Total Hours:_____

Check any defective item and explain in the notes section below:

| | | | |
|---|---|---|---|
| | Accelerator | | Hour Meter |
| | Alarms | | Hydraulic Controls |
| | Battery Connector | | Lights - Head and Tail |
| | Battery - Discharge Indicator | | Lights - Warning |
| | Belt | | Mast |
| | Brakes - Parking | | Oil Leaks |
| | Brakes - Service | | Oil Pressure |
| | Cables | | Overhead Guard |
| | Engine Oil Level | | Radiator Level |
| | Forks | | Safety Equipment |
| | Fuel | | Steering |
| | Gauges | | Tires |
| | Horn | | Unusual Noises |
| | Hoses | | Other _____ |

Notes:_____

_____

_____

_____

_____

_____

_____

_____

_____

_____

Operator's Name:_____

Operator's Signature:_____

Supervisor's Name:_____

Supervisor's Signature:_____

Date: _____ Shift: _____

Truck Number: _____ Electric: ___ Internal Combustion: ___

Hour Meter Start: _____ End: _____ Total Hours: _____

Check any defective item and explain in the notes section below:

| | | | |
|---|---|---|---|
| | Accelerator | | Hour Meter |
| | Alarms | | Hydraulic Controls |
| | Battery Connector | | Lights - Head and Tail |
| | Battery - Discharge Indicator | | Lights - Warning |
| | Belt | | Mast |
| | Brakes - Parking | | Oil Leaks |
| | Brakes - Service | | Oil Pressure |
| | Cables | | Overhead Guard |
| | Engine Oil Level | | Radiator Level |
| | Forks | | Safety Equipment |
| | Fuel | | Steering |
| | Gauges | | Tires |
| | Horn | | Unusual Noises |
| | Hoses | | Other _____ |

Notes:_____
_____
_____
_____
_____
_____
_____
_____
_____

Operator's Name:_____

Operator's Signature:_____

Supervisor's Name:_____

Supervisor's Signature:_____

Date: _____  Shift: _____

Truck Number: _____  Electric: ____  Internal Combustion: ____

Hour Meter Start: _____  End: _____  Total Hours: _____

Check any defective item and explain in the notes section below:

| | | | |
|---|---|---|---|
| | Accelerator | | Hour Meter |
| | Alarms | | Hydraulic Controls |
| | Battery Connector | | Lights - Head and Tail |
| | Battery - Discharge Indicator | | Lights - Warning |
| | Belt | | Mast |
| | Brakes - Parking | | Oil Leaks |
| | Brakes - Service | | Oil Pressure |
| | Cables | | Overhead Guard |
| | Engine Oil Level | | Radiator Level |
| | Forks | | Safety Equipment |
| | Fuel | | Steering |
| | Gauges | | Tires |
| | Horn | | Unusual Noises |
| | Hoses | | Other _____ |

Notes: _____

_____

_____

_____

_____

_____

_____

_____

_____

_____

Operator's Name: _____

Operator's Signature: _____

Supervisor's Name: _____

Supervisor's Signature: _____

Date: _____   Shift: _____

Truck Number:_____ Electric:____ Internal Combustion:____

Hour Meter Start:_____ End:_____ Total Hours:_____

Check any defective item and explain in the notes section below:

| |  | |  |
|---|---|---|---|
| | Accelerator | | Hour Meter |
| | Alarms | | Hydraulic Controls |
| | Battery Connector | | Lights - Head and Tail |
| | Battery - Discharge Indicator | | Lights - Warning |
| | Belt | | Mast |
| | Brakes - Parking | | Oil Leaks |
| | Brakes - Service | | Oil Pressure |
| | Cables | | Overhead Guard |
| | Engine Oil Level | | Radiator Level |
| | Forks | | Safety Equipment |
| | Fuel | | Steering |
| | Gauges | | Tires |
| | Horn | | Unusual Noises |
| | Hoses | | Other _____ |

Notes:_____

_____

_____

_____

_____

_____

_____

_____

_____

Operator's Name:_____

Operator's Signature:_____

Supervisor's Name:_____

Supervisor's Signature:_____

Date: _____ Shift: _____

Truck Number:_____ Electric:____ Internal Combustion:____

Hour Meter Start:_____ End:_____ Total Hours:_____

Check any defective item and explain in the notes section below:

| | | | |
|---|---|---|---|
| | Accelerator | | Hour Meter |
| | Alarms | | Hydraulic Controls |
| | Battery Connector | | Lights - Head and Tail |
| | Battery - Discharge Indicator | | Lights - Warning |
| | Belt | | Mast |
| | Brakes - Parking | | Oil Leaks |
| | Brakes - Service | | Oil Pressure |
| | Cables | | Overhead Guard |
| | Engine Oil Level | | Radiator Level |
| | Forks | | Safety Equipment |
| | Fuel | | Steering |
| | Gauges | | Tires |
| | Horn | | Unusual Noises |
| | Hoses | | Other _____ |

Notes:_____

_____

_____

_____

_____

_____

_____

_____

_____

Operator's Name:_____

Operator's Signature:_____

Supervisor's Name:_____

Supervisor's Signature:_____

Date: _____ Shift: _____

Truck Number:_____ Electric:____ Internal Combustion:____

Hour Meter Start:_____ End:_____ Total Hours:_____

Check any defective item and explain in the notes section below:

| | | | |
|---|---|---|---|
| | Accelerator | | Hour Meter |
| | Alarms | | Hydraulic Controls |
| | Battery Connector | | Lights - Head and Tail |
| | Battery - Discharge Indicator | | Lights - Warning |
| | Belt | | Mast |
| | Brakes - Parking | | Oil Leaks |
| | Brakes - Service | | Oil Pressure |
| | Cables | | Overhead Guard |
| | Engine Oil Level | | Radiator Level |
| | Forks | | Safety Equipment |
| | Fuel | | Steering |
| | Gauges | | Tires |
| | Horn | | Unusual Noises |
| | Hoses | | Other _____ |

Notes:_____

_____

_____

_____

_____

_____

_____

_____

_____

Operator's Name:_____

Operator's Signature:_____

Supervisor's Name:_____

Supervisor's Signature:_____

Date: _____ Shift: _____

Truck Number:_____ Electric:____ Internal Combustion:____

Hour Meter Start:_____ End:_____ Total Hours:_____

Check any defective item and explain in the notes section below:

| | | | |
|---|---|---|---|
| | Accelerator | | Hour Meter |
| | Alarms | | Hydraulic Controls |
| | Battery Connector | | Lights - Head and Tail |
| | Battery - Discharge Indicator | | Lights - Warning |
| | Belt | | Mast |
| | Brakes - Parking | | Oil Leaks |
| | Brakes - Service | | Oil Pressure |
| | Cables | | Overhead Guard |
| | Engine Oil Level | | Radiator Level |
| | Forks | | Safety Equipment |
| | Fuel | | Steering |
| | Gauges | | Tires |
| | Horn | | Unusual Noises |
| | Hoses | | Other _____ |

Notes:_____

_____

_____

_____

_____

_____

_____

_____

_____

Operator's Name:_____

Operator's Signature:_____

Supervisor's Name:_____

Supervisor's Signature:_____

Date: _____ Shift: _____

Truck Number:_____ Electric:___ Internal Combustion:___

Hour Meter Start:_____ End:_____ Total Hours:_____

Check any defective item and explain in the notes section below:

| | | | |
|---|---|---|---|
| | Accelerator | | Hour Meter |
| | Alarms | | Hydraulic Controls |
| | Battery Connector | | Lights - Head and Tail |
| | Battery - Discharge Indicator | | Lights - Warning |
| | Belt | | Mast |
| | Brakes - Parking | | Oil Leaks |
| | Brakes - Service | | Oil Pressure |
| | Cables | | Overhead Guard |
| | Engine Oil Level | | Radiator Level |
| | Forks | | Safety Equipment |
| | Fuel | | Steering |
| | Gauges | | Tires |
| | Horn | | Unusual Noises |
| | Hoses | | Other _____ |

Notes:_____
_____
_____
_____
_____
_____
_____
_____
_____

Operator's Name:_____

Operator's Signature:_____

Supervisor's Name:_____

Supervisor's Signature:_____

Date: _____ Shift: _____

Truck Number:_____ Electric:____ Internal Combustion:____

Hour Meter Start:_____ End:_____ Total Hours:_____

Check any defective item and explain in the notes section below:

| | | | |
|---|---|---|---|
| | Accelerator | | Hour Meter |
| | Alarms | | Hydraulic Controls |
| | Battery Connector | | Lights - Head and Tail |
| | Battery - Discharge Indicator | | Lights - Warning |
| | Belt | | Mast |
| | Brakes - Parking | | Oil Leaks |
| | Brakes - Service | | Oil Pressure |
| | Cables | | Overhead Guard |
| | Engine Oil Level | | Radiator Level |
| | Forks | | Safety Equipment |
| | Fuel | | Steering |
| | Gauges | | Tires |
| | Horn | | Unusual Noises |
| | Hoses | | Other _____ |

Notes:_____

_____

_____

_____

_____

_____

_____

_____

_____

Operator's Name:_____

Operator's Signature:_____

Supervisor's Name:_____

Supervisor's Signature:_____

Date: _____ Shift: _____

Truck Number:_____ Electric:___ Internal Combustion:___

Hour Meter Start:_____ End:_____ Total Hours:_____

Check any defective item and explain in the notes section below:

| | | | |
|---|---|---|---|
| | Accelerator | | Hour Meter |
| | Alarms | | Hydraulic Controls |
| | Battery Connector | | Lights - Head and Tail |
| | Battery - Discharge Indicator | | Lights - Warning |
| | Belt | | Mast |
| | Brakes - Parking | | Oil Leaks |
| | Brakes - Service | | Oil Pressure |
| | Cables | | Overhead Guard |
| | Engine Oil Level | | Radiator Level |
| | Forks | | Safety Equipment |
| | Fuel | | Steering |
| | Gauges | | Tires |
| | Horn | | Unusual Noises |
| | Hoses | | Other _____ |

Notes:_____
_____
_____
_____
_____
_____
_____
_____
_____

Operator's Name:_____

Operator's Signature:_____

Supervisor's Name:_____

Supervisor's Signature:_____

Date: _____     Shift: _____

Truck Number:_____ Electric:____ Internal Combustion:____

Hour Meter Start:_____ End:_____ Total Hours:_____

Check any defective item and explain in the notes section below:

| | | | |
|---|---|---|---|
| | Accelerator | | Hour Meter |
| | Alarms | | Hydraulic Controls |
| | Battery Connector | | Lights - Head and Tail |
| | Battery - Discharge Indicator | | Lights - Warning |
| | Belt | | Mast |
| | Brakes - Parking | | Oil Leaks |
| | Brakes - Service | | Oil Pressure |
| | Cables | | Overhead Guard |
| | Engine Oil Level | | Radiator Level |
| | Forks | | Safety Equipment |
| | Fuel | | Steering |
| | Gauges | | Tires |
| | Horn | | Unusual Noises |
| | Hoses | | Other _____ |

Notes:_____

_____
_____
_____
_____
_____
_____
_____
_____

Operator's Name:_____

Operator's Signature:_____

Supervisor's Name:_____

Supervisor's Signature:_____

Date: _____ Shift: _____

Truck Number:_____ Electric:____ Internal Combustion:____

Hour Meter Start:_____ End:_____ Total Hours:_____

Check any defective item and explain in the notes section below:

| | | | |
|---|---|---|---|
| | Accelerator | | Hour Meter |
| | Alarms | | Hydraulic Controls |
| | Battery Connector | | Lights - Head and Tail |
| | Battery - Discharge Indicator | | Lights - Warning |
| | Belt | | Mast |
| | Brakes - Parking | | Oil Leaks |
| | Brakes - Service | | Oil Pressure |
| | Cables | | Overhead Guard |
| | Engine Oil Level | | Radiator Level |
| | Forks | | Safety Equipment |
| | Fuel | | Steering |
| | Gauges | | Tires |
| | Horn | | Unusual Noises |
| | Hoses | | Other _____ |

Notes:_____

_____

_____

_____

_____

_____

_____

_____

_____

Operator's Name:_____

Operator's Signature:_____

Supervisor's Name:_____

Supervisor's Signature:_____

Date: _____ Shift: _____

Truck Number:_____ Electric:____ Internal Combustion:____

Hour Meter Start:_____ End:_____ Total Hours:_____

Check any defective item and explain in the notes section below:

| | | | |
|---|---|---|---|
| | Accelerator | | Hour Meter |
| | Alarms | | Hydraulic Controls |
| | Battery Connector | | Lights - Head and Tail |
| | Battery - Discharge Indicator | | Lights - Warning |
| | Belt | | Mast |
| | Brakes - Parking | | Oil Leaks |
| | Brakes - Service | | Oil Pressure |
| | Cables | | Overhead Guard |
| | Engine Oil Level | | Radiator Level |
| | Forks | | Safety Equipment |
| | Fuel | | Steering |
| | Gauges | | Tires |
| | Horn | | Unusual Noises |
| | Hoses | | Other _____ |

Notes:_____

_____

_____

_____

_____

_____

_____

_____

_____

_____

Operator's Name:_____

Operator's Signature:_____

Supervisor's Name:_____

Supervisor's Signature:_____

Date: _____  Shift: _____

Truck Number:_____ Electric:____ Internal Combustion:____

Hour Meter Start:_____ End:_____ Total Hours:_____

Check any defective item and explain in the notes section below:

| | | | |
|---|---|---|---|
| | Accelerator | | Hour Meter |
| | Alarms | | Hydraulic Controls |
| | Battery Connector | | Lights - Head and Tail |
| | Battery - Discharge Indicator | | Lights - Warning |
| | Belt | | Mast |
| | Brakes - Parking | | Oil Leaks |
| | Brakes - Service | | Oil Pressure |
| | Cables | | Overhead Guard |
| | Engine Oil Level | | Radiator Level |
| | Forks | | Safety Equipment |
| | Fuel | | Steering |
| | Gauges | | Tires |
| | Horn | | Unusual Noises |
| | Hoses | | Other _____ |

Notes:_____

_____

_____

_____

_____

_____

_____

_____

_____

Operator's Name:_____

Operator's Signature:_____

Supervisor's Name:_____

Supervisor's Signature:_____

Date: _____ Shift: _____

Truck Number:_____ Electric:____ Internal Combustion:____

Hour Meter Start:_____ End:_____ Total Hours:_____

Check any defective item and explain in the notes section below:

| | | | |
|---|---|---|---|
| | Accelerator | | Hour Meter |
| | Alarms | | Hydraulic Controls |
| | Battery Connector | | Lights - Head and Tail |
| | Battery - Discharge Indicator | | Lights - Warning |
| | Belt | | Mast |
| | Brakes - Parking | | Oil Leaks |
| | Brakes - Service | | Oil Pressure |
| | Cables | | Overhead Guard |
| | Engine Oil Level | | Radiator Level |
| | Forks | | Safety Equipment |
| | Fuel | | Steering |
| | Gauges | | Tires |
| | Horn | | Unusual Noises |
| | Hoses | | Other _____ |

Notes:_____

_____

_____

_____

_____

_____

_____

_____

_____

_____

Operator's Name:_____

Operator's Signature:_____

Supervisor's Name:_____

Supervisor's Signature:_____

Date: _____ Shift: _____

Truck Number:_____ Electric:___ Internal Combustion:___

Hour Meter Start:_____ End:_____ Total Hours:_____

Check any defective item and explain in the notes section below:

| | | | |
|---|---|---|---|
| | Accelerator | | Hour Meter |
| | Alarms | | Hydraulic Controls |
| | Battery Connector | | Lights - Head and Tail |
| | Battery - Discharge Indicator | | Lights - Warning |
| | Belt | | Mast |
| | Brakes - Parking | | Oil Leaks |
| | Brakes - Service | | Oil Pressure |
| | Cables | | Overhead Guard |
| | Engine Oil Level | | Radiator Level |
| | Forks | | Safety Equipment |
| | Fuel | | Steering |
| | Gauges | | Tires |
| | Horn | | Unusual Noises |
| | Hoses | | Other _____ |

Notes:_____

_____

_____

_____

_____

_____

_____

_____

_____

Operator's Name:_____

Operator's Signature:_____

Supervisor's Name:_____

Supervisor's Signature:_____

Date: _____ Shift: _____

Truck Number:_____ Electric:___ Internal Combustion:___

Hour Meter Start:_____ End:_____ Total Hours:_____

Check any defective item and explain in the notes section below:

| | | | |
|---|---|---|---|
| | Accelerator | | Hour Meter |
| | Alarms | | Hydraulic Controls |
| | Battery Connector | | Lights - Head and Tail |
| | Battery - Discharge Indicator | | Lights - Warning |
| | Belt | | Mast |
| | Brakes - Parking | | Oil Leaks |
| | Brakes - Service | | Oil Pressure |
| | Cables | | Overhead Guard |
| | Engine Oil Level | | Radiator Level |
| | Forks | | Safety Equipment |
| | Fuel | | Steering |
| | Gauges | | Tires |
| | Horn | | Unusual Noises |
| | Hoses | | Other _____ |

Notes:_____

_____

_____

_____

_____

_____

_____

_____

_____

Operator's Name:_____

Operator's Signature:_____

Supervisor's Name:_____

Supervisor's Signature:_____

Date: _____  Shift: _____

Truck Number: _____  Electric: ___  Internal Combustion: ___

Hour Meter Start: _____  End: _____  Total Hours: _____

Check any defective item and explain in the notes section below:

| | | | |
|---|---|---|---|
| | Accelerator | | Hour Meter |
| | Alarms | | Hydraulic Controls |
| | Battery Connector | | Lights - Head and Tail |
| | Battery - Discharge Indicator | | Lights - Warning |
| | Belt | | Mast |
| | Brakes - Parking | | Oil Leaks |
| | Brakes - Service | | Oil Pressure |
| | Cables | | Overhead Guard |
| | Engine Oil Level | | Radiator Level |
| | Forks | | Safety Equipment |
| | Fuel | | Steering |
| | Gauges | | Tires |
| | Horn | | Unusual Noises |
| | Hoses | | Other _____ |

Notes: _____

_____

_____

_____

_____

_____

_____

_____

_____

Operator's Name: _____

Operator's Signature: _____

Supervisor's Name: _____

Supervisor's Signature: _____

Date: _____ Shift: _____

Truck Number: _____ Electric: ____ Internal Combustion: ____

Hour Meter Start: _____ End: _____ Total Hours: _____

Check any defective item and explain in the notes section below:

| | | | |
|---|---|---|---|
| | Accelerator | | Hour Meter |
| | Alarms | | Hydraulic Controls |
| | Battery Connector | | Lights - Head and Tail |
| | Battery - Discharge Indicator | | Lights - Warning |
| | Belt | | Mast |
| | Brakes - Parking | | Oil Leaks |
| | Brakes - Service | | Oil Pressure |
| | Cables | | Overhead Guard |
| | Engine Oil Level | | Radiator Level |
| | Forks | | Safety Equipment |
| | Fuel | | Steering |
| | Gauges | | Tires |
| | Horn | | Unusual Noises |
| | Hoses | | Other _____ |

Notes: _____

_____

_____

_____

_____

_____

_____

_____

_____

Operator's Name: _____

Operator's Signature: _____

Supervisor's Name: _____

Supervisor's Signature: _____

Date: _____ Shift: _____

Truck Number:_____ Electric:____ Internal Combustion:____

Hour Meter Start:_____ End:_____ Total Hours:_____

Check any defective item and explain in the notes section below:

| | | | |
|---|---|---|---|
| | Accelerator | | Hour Meter |
| | Alarms | | Hydraulic Controls |
| | Battery Connector | | Lights - Head and Tail |
| | Battery - Discharge Indicator | | Lights - Warning |
| | Belt | | Mast |
| | Brakes - Parking | | Oil Leaks |
| | Brakes - Service | | Oil Pressure |
| | Cables | | Overhead Guard |
| | Engine Oil Level | | Radiator Level |
| | Forks | | Safety Equipment |
| | Fuel | | Steering |
| | Gauges | | Tires |
| | Horn | | Unusual Noises |
| | Hoses | | Other _____ |

Notes:_____

_____

_____

_____

_____

_____

_____

_____

_____

Operator's Name:_____

Operator's Signature:_____

Supervisor's Name:_____

Supervisor's Signature:_____

Date: _____ Shift: _____

Truck Number:_____ Electric:____ Internal Combustion:____

Hour Meter Start:_____ End:_____ Total Hours:_____

Check any defective item and explain in the notes section below:

|  | | | |
|---|---|---|---|
|  | Accelerator | | Hour Meter |
|  | Alarms | | Hydraulic Controls |
|  | Battery Connector | | Lights - Head and Tail |
|  | Battery - Discharge Indicator | | Lights - Warning |
|  | Belt | | Mast |
|  | Brakes - Parking | | Oil Leaks |
|  | Brakes - Service | | Oil Pressure |
|  | Cables | | Overhead Guard |
|  | Engine Oil Level | | Radiator Level |
|  | Forks | | Safety Equipment |
|  | Fuel | | Steering |
|  | Gauges | | Tires |
|  | Horn | | Unusual Noises |
|  | Hoses | | Other _____ |

Notes:_____

_____

_____

_____

_____

_____

_____

_____

_____

Operator's Name:_____

Operator's Signature:_____

Supervisor's Name:_____

Supervisor's Signature:_____

Date: _____ Shift: _____

Truck Number: _____ Electric: ___ Internal Combustion: ___

Hour Meter Start: _____ End: _____ Total Hours: _____

Check any defective item and explain in the notes section below:

| | | | |
|---|---|---|---|
| | Accelerator | | Hour Meter |
| | Alarms | | Hydraulic Controls |
| | Battery Connector | | Lights - Head and Tail |
| | Battery - Discharge Indicator | | Lights - Warning |
| | Belt | | Mast |
| | Brakes - Parking | | Oil Leaks |
| | Brakes - Service | | Oil Pressure |
| | Cables | | Overhead Guard |
| | Engine Oil Level | | Radiator Level |
| | Forks | | Safety Equipment |
| | Fuel | | Steering |
| | Gauges | | Tires |
| | Horn | | Unusual Noises |
| | Hoses | | Other _____ |

Notes: _____
_____
_____
_____
_____
_____
_____
_____
_____

Operator's Name: _____

Operator's Signature: _____

Supervisor's Name: _____

Supervisor's Signature: _____

Date: _____ Shift: _____

Truck Number: _____ Electric: ___ Internal Combustion: ___

Hour Meter Start: _____ End: _____ Total Hours: _____

Check any defective item and explain in the notes section below:

| | | | |
|---|---|---|---|
| | Accelerator | | Hour Meter |
| | Alarms | | Hydraulic Controls |
| | Battery Connector | | Lights - Head and Tail |
| | Battery - Discharge Indicator | | Lights - Warning |
| | Belt | | Mast |
| | Brakes - Parking | | Oil Leaks |
| | Brakes - Service | | Oil Pressure |
| | Cables | | Overhead Guard |
| | Engine Oil Level | | Radiator Level |
| | Forks | | Safety Equipment |
| | Fuel | | Steering |
| | Gauges | | Tires |
| | Horn | | Unusual Noises |
| | Hoses | | Other _____ |

Notes: _____
_____
_____
_____
_____
_____
_____
_____
_____
_____

Operator's Name: _____

Operator's Signature: _____

Supervisor's Name: _____

Supervisor's Signature: _____

Date: _____ Shift: _____

Truck Number:_____ Electric:____ Internal Combustion:____

Hour Meter Start:_____ End:_____ Total Hours:_____

Check any defective item and explain in the notes section below:

| | | | |
|---|---|---|---|
| | Accelerator | | Hour Meter |
| | Alarms | | Hydraulic Controls |
| | Battery Connector | | Lights - Head and Tail |
| | Battery - Discharge Indicator | | Lights - Warning |
| | Belt | | Mast |
| | Brakes - Parking | | Oil Leaks |
| | Brakes - Service | | Oil Pressure |
| | Cables | | Overhead Guard |
| | Engine Oil Level | | Radiator Level |
| | Forks | | Safety Equipment |
| | Fuel | | Steering |
| | Gauges | | Tires |
| | Horn | | Unusual Noises |
| | Hoses | | Other _____ |

Notes:_____

_____

_____

_____

_____

_____

_____

_____

_____

Operator's Name:_____

Operator's Signature:_____

Supervisor's Name:_____

Supervisor's Signature:_____

Date: _____ Shift: _____

Truck Number:_____ Electric:___ Internal Combustion:___

Hour Meter Start:_____ End:_____ Total Hours:_____

Check any defective item and explain in the notes section below:

| | | | |
|---|---|---|---|
| | Accelerator | | Hour Meter |
| | Alarms | | Hydraulic Controls |
| | Battery Connector | | Lights - Head and Tail |
| | Battery - Discharge Indicator | | Lights - Warning |
| | Belt | | Mast |
| | Brakes - Parking | | Oil Leaks |
| | Brakes - Service | | Oil Pressure |
| | Cables | | Overhead Guard |
| | Engine Oil Level | | Radiator Level |
| | Forks | | Safety Equipment |
| | Fuel | | Steering |
| | Gauges | | Tires |
| | Horn | | Unusual Noises |
| | Hoses | | Other _____ |

Notes:_____

_____

_____

_____

_____

_____

_____

_____

_____

_____

Operator's Name:_____

Operator's Signature:_____

Supervisor's Name:_____

Supervisor's Signature:_____

Date: _____ Shift: _____

Truck Number:_____ Electric:___ Internal Combustion:___

Hour Meter Start:_____ End:_____ Total Hours:_____

Check any defective item and explain in the notes section below:

|  | Accelerator |  | Hour Meter |
|---|---|---|---|
|  | Alarms |  | Hydraulic Controls |
|  | Battery Connector |  | Lights - Head and Tail |
|  | Battery - Discharge Indicator |  | Lights - Warning |
|  | Belt |  | Mast |
|  | Brakes - Parking |  | Oil Leaks |
|  | Brakes - Service |  | Oil Pressure |
|  | Cables |  | Overhead Guard |
|  | Engine Oil Level |  | Radiator Level |
|  | Forks |  | Safety Equipment |
|  | Fuel |  | Steering |
|  | Gauges |  | Tires |
|  | Horn |  | Unusual Noises |
|  | Hoses |  | Other _____ |

Notes:_____

_____

_____

_____

_____

_____

_____

_____

_____

Operator's Name:_____

Operator's Signature:_____

Supervisor's Name:_____

Supervisor's Signature:_____

Date: _____  Shift: _____

Truck Number:_____ Electric:____ Internal Combustion:____

Hour Meter Start:_____ End:_____ Total Hours:_____

Check any defective item and explain in the notes section below:

| | | | |
|---|---|---|---|
| | Accelerator | | Hour Meter |
| | Alarms | | Hydraulic Controls |
| | Battery Connector | | Lights - Head and Tail |
| | Battery - Discharge Indicator | | Lights - Warning |
| | Belt | | Mast |
| | Brakes - Parking | | Oil Leaks |
| | Brakes - Service | | Oil Pressure |
| | Cables | | Overhead Guard |
| | Engine Oil Level | | Radiator Level |
| | Forks | | Safety Equipment |
| | Fuel | | Steering |
| | Gauges | | Tires |
| | Horn | | Unusual Noises |
| | Hoses | | Other _____ |

Notes:_____

_____

_____

_____

_____

_____

_____

_____

_____

Operator's Name:_____

Operator's Signature:_____

Supervisor's Name:_____

Supervisor's Signature:_____

Date: _____ Shift: _____

Truck Number:_____ Electric:____ Internal Combustion:____

Hour Meter Start:_____ End:_____ Total Hours:_____

Check any defective item and explain in the notes section below:

| | | | |
|---|---|---|---|
| | Accelerator | | Hour Meter |
| | Alarms | | Hydraulic Controls |
| | Battery Connector | | Lights - Head and Tail |
| | Battery - Discharge Indicator | | Lights - Warning |
| | Belt | | Mast |
| | Brakes - Parking | | Oil Leaks |
| | Brakes - Service | | Oil Pressure |
| | Cables | | Overhead Guard |
| | Engine Oil Level | | Radiator Level |
| | Forks | | Safety Equipment |
| | Fuel | | Steering |
| | Gauges | | Tires |
| | Horn | | Unusual Noises |
| | Hoses | | Other _____ |

Notes:_____

_____

_____

_____

_____

_____

_____

_____

_____

Operator's Name:_____

Operator's Signature:_____

Supervisor's Name:_____

Supervisor's Signature:_____

Date: _____ Shift: _____

Truck Number:_____ Electric:____ Internal Combustion:____

Hour Meter Start:_____ End:_____ Total Hours:_____

Check any defective item and explain in the notes section below:

| | | | |
|---|---|---|---|
| | Accelerator | | Hour Meter |
| | Alarms | | Hydraulic Controls |
| | Battery Connector | | Lights - Head and Tail |
| | Battery - Discharge Indicator | | Lights - Warning |
| | Belt | | Mast |
| | Brakes - Parking | | Oil Leaks |
| | Brakes - Service | | Oil Pressure |
| | Cables | | Overhead Guard |
| | Engine Oil Level | | Radiator Level |
| | Forks | | Safety Equipment |
| | Fuel | | Steering |
| | Gauges | | Tires |
| | Horn | | Unusual Noises |
| | Hoses | | Other _____ |

Notes:_____

_____

_____

_____

_____

_____

_____

_____

_____

Operator's Name:_____

Operator's Signature:_____

Supervisor's Name:_____

Supervisor's Signature:_____

Date: _____ Shift: _____

Truck Number:_____ Electric:____ Internal Combustion:____

Hour Meter Start:_____ End:_____ Total Hours:_____

Check any defective item and explain in the notes section below:

| | | | |
|---|---|---|---|
| | Accelerator | | Hour Meter |
| | Alarms | | Hydraulic Controls |
| | Battery Connector | | Lights - Head and Tail |
| | Battery - Discharge Indicator | | Lights - Warning |
| | Belt | | Mast |
| | Brakes - Parking | | Oil Leaks |
| | Brakes - Service | | Oil Pressure |
| | Cables | | Overhead Guard |
| | Engine Oil Level | | Radiator Level |
| | Forks | | Safety Equipment |
| | Fuel | | Steering |
| | Gauges | | Tires |
| | Horn | | Unusual Noises |
| | Hoses | | Other _____ |

Notes:_____

_____

_____

_____

_____

_____

_____

_____

_____

_____

Operator's Name:_____

Operator's Signature:_____

Supervisor's Name:_____

Supervisor's Signature:_____

Date: _____ Shift: _____

Truck Number:_____ Electric:___ Internal Combustion:___

Hour Meter Start:_____ End:_____ Total Hours:_____

Check any defective item and explain in the notes section below:

| | | | |
|---|---|---|---|
| | Accelerator | | Hour Meter |
| | Alarms | | Hydraulic Controls |
| | Battery Connector | | Lights - Head and Tail |
| | Battery - Discharge Indicator | | Lights - Warning |
| | Belt | | Mast |
| | Brakes - Parking | | Oil Leaks |
| | Brakes - Service | | Oil Pressure |
| | Cables | | Overhead Guard |
| | Engine Oil Level | | Radiator Level |
| | Forks | | Safety Equipment |
| | Fuel | | Steering |
| | Gauges | | Tires |
| | Horn | | Unusual Noises |
| | Hoses | | Other _____ |

Notes:_____

_____

_____

_____

_____

_____

_____

_____

_____

_____

Operator's Name:_____

Operator's Signature:_____

Supervisor's Name:_____

Supervisor's Signature:_____

Date: _____ Shift: _____

Truck Number: _____ Electric: ____ Internal Combustion: ____

Hour Meter Start: _____ End: _____ Total Hours: _____

Check any defective item and explain in the notes section below:

| | | | |
|---|---|---|---|
| | Accelerator | | Hour Meter |
| | Alarms | | Hydraulic Controls |
| | Battery Connector | | Lights - Head and Tail |
| | Battery - Discharge Indicator | | Lights - Warning |
| | Belt | | Mast |
| | Brakes - Parking | | Oil Leaks |
| | Brakes - Service | | Oil Pressure |
| | Cables | | Overhead Guard |
| | Engine Oil Level | | Radiator Level |
| | Forks | | Safety Equipment |
| | Fuel | | Steering |
| | Gauges | | Tires |
| | Horn | | Unusual Noises |
| | Hoses | | Other _____ |

Notes: _____

_____

_____

_____

_____

_____

_____

_____

_____

Operator's Name: _____

Operator's Signature: _____

Supervisor's Name: _____

Supervisor's Signature: _____

Date: _____ Shift: _____

Truck Number:_____ Electric:____ Internal Combustion:____

Hour Meter Start:_____ End:_____ Total Hours:_____

Check any defective item and explain in the notes section below:

| | | | |
|---|---|---|---|
| | Accelerator | | Hour Meter |
| | Alarms | | Hydraulic Controls |
| | Battery Connector | | Lights - Head and Tail |
| | Battery - Discharge Indicator | | Lights - Warning |
| | Belt | | Mast |
| | Brakes - Parking | | Oil Leaks |
| | Brakes - Service | | Oil Pressure |
| | Cables | | Overhead Guard |
| | Engine Oil Level | | Radiator Level |
| | Forks | | Safety Equipment |
| | Fuel | | Steering |
| | Gauges | | Tires |
| | Horn | | Unusual Noises |
| | Hoses | | Other _____ |

Notes:_____

_____

_____

_____

_____

_____

_____

_____

_____

Operator's Name:_____

Operator's Signature:_____

Supervisor's Name:_____

Supervisor's Signature:_____

Date: _____ Shift: _____

Truck Number:_____ Electric:___ Internal Combustion:___

Hour Meter Start:_____ End:_____ Total Hours:_____

Check any defective item and explain in the notes section below:

| | | | |
|---|---|---|---|
| | Accelerator | | Hour Meter |
| | Alarms | | Hydraulic Controls |
| | Battery Connector | | Lights - Head and Tail |
| | Battery - Discharge Indicator | | Lights - Warning |
| | Belt | | Mast |
| | Brakes - Parking | | Oil Leaks |
| | Brakes - Service | | Oil Pressure |
| | Cables | | Overhead Guard |
| | Engine Oil Level | | Radiator Level |
| | Forks | | Safety Equipment |
| | Fuel | | Steering |
| | Gauges | | Tires |
| | Horn | | Unusual Noises |
| | Hoses | | Other _____ |

Notes:_____

_____

_____

_____

_____

_____

_____

_____

_____

Operator's Name:_____

Operator's Signature:_____

Supervisor's Name:_____

Supervisor's Signature:_____

Date: _____ Shift: _____

Truck Number: _____ Electric: ____ Internal Combustion: ____

Hour Meter Start: _____ End: _____ Total Hours: _____

Check any defective item and explain in the notes section below:

| | | | |
|---|---|---|---|
| | Accelerator | | Hour Meter |
| | Alarms | | Hydraulic Controls |
| | Battery Connector | | Lights - Head and Tail |
| | Battery - Discharge Indicator | | Lights - Warning |
| | Belt | | Mast |
| | Brakes - Parking | | Oil Leaks |
| | Brakes - Service | | Oil Pressure |
| | Cables | | Overhead Guard |
| | Engine Oil Level | | Radiator Level |
| | Forks | | Safety Equipment |
| | Fuel | | Steering |
| | Gauges | | Tires |
| | Horn | | Unusual Noises |
| | Hoses | | Other _____ |

Notes: _____

_____

_____

_____

_____

_____

_____

_____

_____

Operator's Name: _____

Operator's Signature: _____

Supervisor's Name: _____

Supervisor's Signature: _____

Date: _____ Shift: _____

Truck Number:_____ Electric:____ Internal Combustion:____

Hour Meter Start:_____ End:_____ Total Hours:_____

Check any defective item and explain in the notes section below:

| | | | |
|---|---|---|---|
| | Accelerator | | Hour Meter |
| | Alarms | | Hydraulic Controls |
| | Battery Connector | | Lights - Head and Tail |
| | Battery - Discharge Indicator | | Lights - Warning |
| | Belt | | Mast |
| | Brakes - Parking | | Oil Leaks |
| | Brakes - Service | | Oil Pressure |
| | Cables | | Overhead Guard |
| | Engine Oil Level | | Radiator Level |
| | Forks | | Safety Equipment |
| | Fuel | | Steering |
| | Gauges | | Tires |
| | Horn | | Unusual Noises |
| | Hoses | | Other _____ |

Notes:_____

_____

_____

_____

_____

_____

_____

_____

_____

Operator's Name:_____

Operator's Signature:_____

Supervisor's Name:_____

Supervisor's Signature:_____

Date: _____ Shift: _____

Truck Number:_____ Electric:____ Internal Combustion:____

Hour Meter Start:_____ End:_____ Total Hours:_____

Check any defective item and explain in the notes section below:

| | | | |
|---|---|---|---|
| | Accelerator | | Hour Meter |
| | Alarms | | Hydraulic Controls |
| | Battery Connector | | Lights - Head and Tail |
| | Battery - Discharge Indicator | | Lights - Warning |
| | Belt | | Mast |
| | Brakes - Parking | | Oil Leaks |
| | Brakes - Service | | Oil Pressure |
| | Cables | | Overhead Guard |
| | Engine Oil Level | | Radiator Level |
| | Forks | | Safety Equipment |
| | Fuel | | Steering |
| | Gauges | | Tires |
| | Horn | | Unusual Noises |
| | Hoses | | Other _____ |

Notes:_____

_____

_____

_____

_____

_____

_____

_____

_____

Operator's Name:_____

Operator's Signature:_____

Supervisor's Name:_____

Supervisor's Signature:_____

Date: _____ Shift: _____

Truck Number: _____ Electric: ____ Internal Combustion: ____

Hour Meter Start: _____ End: _____ Total Hours: _____

Check any defective item and explain in the notes section below:

| | | | |
|---|---|---|---|
| | Accelerator | | Hour Meter |
| | Alarms | | Hydraulic Controls |
| | Battery Connector | | Lights - Head and Tail |
| | Battery - Discharge Indicator | | Lights - Warning |
| | Belt | | Mast |
| | Brakes - Parking | | Oil Leaks |
| | Brakes - Service | | Oil Pressure |
| | Cables | | Overhead Guard |
| | Engine Oil Level | | Radiator Level |
| | Forks | | Safety Equipment |
| | Fuel | | Steering |
| | Gauges | | Tires |
| | Horn | | Unusual Noises |
| | Hoses | | Other _____ |

Notes: _____
_____
_____
_____
_____
_____
_____
_____
_____
_____

Operator's Name: _____

Operator's Signature: _____

Supervisor's Name: _____

Supervisor's Signature: _____

Date: _____ Shift: _____

Truck Number:_____ Electric:___ Internal Combustion:___

Hour Meter Start:_____ End:_____ Total Hours:_____

Check any defective item and explain in the notes section below:

| | | | |
|---|---|---|---|
| | Accelerator | | Hour Meter |
| | Alarms | | Hydraulic Controls |
| | Battery Connector | | Lights - Head and Tail |
| | Battery - Discharge Indicator | | Lights - Warning |
| | Belt | | Mast |
| | Brakes - Parking | | Oil Leaks |
| | Brakes - Service | | Oil Pressure |
| | Cables | | Overhead Guard |
| | Engine Oil Level | | Radiator Level |
| | Forks | | Safety Equipment |
| | Fuel | | Steering |
| | Gauges | | Tires |
| | Horn | | Unusual Noises |
| | Hoses | | Other _____ |

Notes:_____

_____

_____

_____

_____

_____

_____

_____

_____

Operator's Name:_____

Operator's Signature:_____

Supervisor's Name:_____

Supervisor's Signature:_____

Date: _____ Shift: _____

Truck Number:_____ Electric:____ Internal Combustion:____

Hour Meter Start:_____ End:_____ Total Hours:_____

Check any defective item and explain in the notes section below:

| | | | |
|---|---|---|---|
| | Accelerator | | Hour Meter |
| | Alarms | | Hydraulic Controls |
| | Battery Connector | | Lights - Head and Tail |
| | Battery - Discharge Indicator | | Lights - Warning |
| | Belt | | Mast |
| | Brakes - Parking | | Oil Leaks |
| | Brakes - Service | | Oil Pressure |
| | Cables | | Overhead Guard |
| | Engine Oil Level | | Radiator Level |
| | Forks | | Safety Equipment |
| | Fuel | | Steering |
| | Gauges | | Tires |
| | Horn | | Unusual Noises |
| | Hoses | | Other _____ |

Notes:_____

_____

_____

_____

_____

_____

_____

_____

_____

Operator's Name:_____

Operator's Signature:_____

Supervisor's Name:_____

Supervisor's Signature:_____

Date: _____ Shift: _____

Truck Number:_____ Electric:____ Internal Combustion:____

Hour Meter Start:_____ End:_____ Total Hours:_____

Check any defective item and explain in the notes section below:

| | | | |
|---|---|---|---|
| | Accelerator | | Hour Meter |
| | Alarms | | Hydraulic Controls |
| | Battery Connector | | Lights - Head and Tail |
| | Battery - Discharge Indicator | | Lights - Warning |
| | Belt | | Mast |
| | Brakes - Parking | | Oil Leaks |
| | Brakes - Service | | Oil Pressure |
| | Cables | | Overhead Guard |
| | Engine Oil Level | | Radiator Level |
| | Forks | | Safety Equipment |
| | Fuel | | Steering |
| | Gauges | | Tires |
| | Horn | | Unusual Noises |
| | Hoses | | Other _____ |

Notes:_____

_____

_____

_____

_____

_____

_____

_____

_____

_____

Operator's Name:_____

Operator's Signature:_____

Supervisor's Name:_____

Supervisor's Signature:_____

Date: _____  Shift: _____

Truck Number:_____  Electric:____  Internal Combustion:____

Hour Meter Start:_____  End:_____  Total Hours:_____

Check any defective item and explain in the notes section below:

| | | | |
|---|---|---|---|
| | Accelerator | | Hour Meter |
| | Alarms | | Hydraulic Controls |
| | Battery Connector | | Lights - Head and Tail |
| | Battery - Discharge Indicator | | Lights - Warning |
| | Belt | | Mast |
| | Brakes - Parking | | Oil Leaks |
| | Brakes - Service | | Oil Pressure |
| | Cables | | Overhead Guard |
| | Engine Oil Level | | Radiator Level |
| | Forks | | Safety Equipment |
| | Fuel | | Steering |
| | Gauges | | Tires |
| | Horn | | Unusual Noises |
| | Hoses | | Other _____ |

Notes:_____

_____

_____

_____

_____

_____

_____

_____

_____

Operator's Name:_____

Operator's Signature:_____

Supervisor's Name:_____

Supervisor's Signature:_____

Date: _____ Shift: _____

Truck Number:_____ Electric:____ Internal Combustion:____

Hour Meter Start:_____ End:_____ Total Hours:_____

Check any defective item and explain in the notes section below:

| | | | |
|---|---|---|---|
| | Accelerator | | Hour Meter |
| | Alarms | | Hydraulic Controls |
| | Battery Connector | | Lights - Head and Tail |
| | Battery - Discharge Indicator | | Lights - Warning |
| | Belt | | Mast |
| | Brakes - Parking | | Oil Leaks |
| | Brakes - Service | | Oil Pressure |
| | Cables | | Overhead Guard |
| | Engine Oil Level | | Radiator Level |
| | Forks | | Safety Equipment |
| | Fuel | | Steering |
| | Gauges | | Tires |
| | Horn | | Unusual Noises |
| | Hoses | | Other _____ |

Notes:_____

_____

_____

_____

_____

_____

_____

_____

_____

Operator's Name:_____

Operator's Signature:_____

Supervisor's Name:_____

Supervisor's Signature:_____

Date: _____ Shift: _____

Truck Number: _____ Electric: ____ Internal Combustion: ____

Hour Meter Start: _____ End: _____ Total Hours: _____

Check any defective item and explain in the notes section below:

| | | | |
|---|---|---|---|
| | Accelerator | | Hour Meter |
| | Alarms | | Hydraulic Controls |
| | Battery Connector | | Lights - Head and Tail |
| | Battery - Discharge Indicator | | Lights - Warning |
| | Belt | | Mast |
| | Brakes - Parking | | Oil Leaks |
| | Brakes - Service | | Oil Pressure |
| | Cables | | Overhead Guard |
| | Engine Oil Level | | Radiator Level |
| | Forks | | Safety Equipment |
| | Fuel | | Steering |
| | Gauges | | Tires |
| | Horn | | Unusual Noises |
| | Hoses | | Other _____ |

Notes: _____

_____

_____

_____

_____

_____

_____

_____

_____

Operator's Name: _____

Operator's Signature: _____

Supervisor's Name: _____

Supervisor's Signature: _____

Date: _____ Shift: _____

Truck Number:_____ Electric:____ Internal Combustion:____

Hour Meter Start:_____ End:_____ Total Hours:_____

Check any defective item and explain in the notes section below:

| | | | |
|---|---|---|---|
| | Accelerator | | Hour Meter |
| | Alarms | | Hydraulic Controls |
| | Battery Connector | | Lights - Head and Tail |
| | Battery - Discharge Indicator | | Lights - Warning |
| | Belt | | Mast |
| | Brakes - Parking | | Oil Leaks |
| | Brakes - Service | | Oil Pressure |
| | Cables | | Overhead Guard |
| | Engine Oil Level | | Radiator Level |
| | Forks | | Safety Equipment |
| | Fuel | | Steering |
| | Gauges | | Tires |
| | Horn | | Unusual Noises |
| | Hoses | | Other _____ |

Notes:_____

_____

_____

_____

_____

_____

_____

_____

_____

Operator's Name:_____

Operator's Signature:_____

Supervisor's Name:_____

Supervisor's Signature:_____

Date: _____  Shift: _____

Truck Number: _____  Electric: ____  Internal Combustion: ____

Hour Meter Start: _____  End: _____  Total Hours: _____

Check any defective item and explain in the notes section below:

| | | | |
|---|---|---|---|
| | Accelerator | | Hour Meter |
| | Alarms | | Hydraulic Controls |
| | Battery Connector | | Lights - Head and Tail |
| | Battery - Discharge Indicator | | Lights - Warning |
| | Belt | | Mast |
| | Brakes - Parking | | Oil Leaks |
| | Brakes - Service | | Oil Pressure |
| | Cables | | Overhead Guard |
| | Engine Oil Level | | Radiator Level |
| | Forks | | Safety Equipment |
| | Fuel | | Steering |
| | Gauges | | Tires |
| | Horn | | Unusual Noises |
| | Hoses | | Other _____ |

Notes: _____
_____
_____
_____
_____
_____
_____
_____
_____

Operator's Name: _____

Operator's Signature: _____

Supervisor's Name: _____

Supervisor's Signature: _____

Date: _____ Shift: _____

Truck Number:_____ Electric:____ Internal Combustion:____

Hour Meter Start:_____ End:_____ Total Hours:_____

Check any defective item and explain in the notes section below:

| | | | |
|---|---|---|---|
| | Accelerator | | Hour Meter |
| | Alarms | | Hydraulic Controls |
| | Battery Connector | | Lights - Head and Tail |
| | Battery - Discharge Indicator | | Lights - Warning |
| | Belt | | Mast |
| | Brakes - Parking | | Oil Leaks |
| | Brakes - Service | | Oil Pressure |
| | Cables | | Overhead Guard |
| | Engine Oil Level | | Radiator Level |
| | Forks | | Safety Equipment |
| | Fuel | | Steering |
| | Gauges | | Tires |
| | Horn | | Unusual Noises |
| | Hoses | | Other _____ |

Notes:_____

_____

_____

_____

_____

_____

_____

_____

_____

_____

Operator's Name:_____

Operator's Signature:_____

Supervisor's Name:_____

Supervisor's Signature:_____

Date: _____ Shift: _____

Truck Number:_____ Electric:___ Internal Combustion:___

Hour Meter Start:_____ End:_____ Total Hours:_____

Check any defective item and explain in the notes section below:

| | | | |
|---|---|---|---|
| | Accelerator | | Hour Meter |
| | Alarms | | Hydraulic Controls |
| | Battery Connector | | Lights - Head and Tail |
| | Battery - Discharge Indicator | | Lights - Warning |
| | Belt | | Mast |
| | Brakes - Parking | | Oil Leaks |
| | Brakes - Service | | Oil Pressure |
| | Cables | | Overhead Guard |
| | Engine Oil Level | | Radiator Level |
| | Forks | | Safety Equipment |
| | Fuel | | Steering |
| | Gauges | | Tires |
| | Horn | | Unusual Noises |
| | Hoses | | Other _____ |

Notes:_____
_____
_____
_____
_____
_____
_____
_____
_____

Operator's Name:_____

Operator's Signature:_____

Supervisor's Name:_____

Supervisor's Signature:_____

Date: _____ Shift: _____

Truck Number:_____ Electric:____ Internal Combustion:____

Hour Meter Start:_____ End:_____ Total Hours:_____

Check any defective item and explain in the notes section below:

| | | | |
|---|---|---|---|
| | Accelerator | | Hour Meter |
| | Alarms | | Hydraulic Controls |
| | Battery Connector | | Lights - Head and Tail |
| | Battery - Discharge Indicator | | Lights - Warning |
| | Belt | | Mast |
| | Brakes - Parking | | Oil Leaks |
| | Brakes - Service | | Oil Pressure |
| | Cables | | Overhead Guard |
| | Engine Oil Level | | Radiator Level |
| | Forks | | Safety Equipment |
| | Fuel | | Steering |
| | Gauges | | Tires |
| | Horn | | Unusual Noises |
| | Hoses | | Other _____ |

Notes:_____

_____

_____

_____

_____

_____

_____

_____

_____

Operator's Name:_____

Operator's Signature:_____

Supervisor's Name:_____

Supervisor's Signature:_____

Date: _____ Shift: _____

Truck Number: _____ Electric: ___ Internal Combustion: ___

Hour Meter Start: _____ End: _____ Total Hours: _____

Check any defective item and explain in the notes section below:

| | | | |
|---|---|---|---|
| | Accelerator | | Hour Meter |
| | Alarms | | Hydraulic Controls |
| | Battery Connector | | Lights - Head and Tail |
| | Battery - Discharge Indicator | | Lights - Warning |
| | Belt | | Mast |
| | Brakes - Parking | | Oil Leaks |
| | Brakes - Service | | Oil Pressure |
| | Cables | | Overhead Guard |
| | Engine Oil Level | | Radiator Level |
| | Forks | | Safety Equipment |
| | Fuel | | Steering |
| | Gauges | | Tires |
| | Horn | | Unusual Noises |
| | Hoses | | Other _____ |

Notes: _____
_____
_____
_____
_____
_____
_____
_____
_____

Operator's Name: _____

Operator's Signature: _____

Supervisor's Name: _____

Supervisor's Signature: _____

Date: _____ Shift: _____

Truck Number:_____ Electric:____ Internal Combustion:____

Hour Meter Start:_____ End:_____ Total Hours:_____

Check any defective item and explain in the notes section below:

| | | | |
|---|---|---|---|
| | Accelerator | | Hour Meter |
| | Alarms | | Hydraulic Controls |
| | Battery Connector | | Lights - Head and Tail |
| | Battery - Discharge Indicator | | Lights - Warning |
| | Belt | | Mast |
| | Brakes - Parking | | Oil Leaks |
| | Brakes - Service | | Oil Pressure |
| | Cables | | Overhead Guard |
| | Engine Oil Level | | Radiator Level |
| | Forks | | Safety Equipment |
| | Fuel | | Steering |
| | Gauges | | Tires |
| | Horn | | Unusual Noises |
| | Hoses | | Other _____ |

Notes:_____

_____

_____

_____

_____

_____

_____

_____

_____

Operator's Name:_____

Operator's Signature:_____

Supervisor's Name:_____

Supervisor's Signature:_____

Date: _____ Shift: _____

Truck Number: _____ Electric: ___ Internal Combustion: ___

Hour Meter Start: _____ End: _____ Total Hours: _____

Check any defective item and explain in the notes section below:

| | | | |
|---|---|---|---|
| | Accelerator | | Hour Meter |
| | Alarms | | Hydraulic Controls |
| | Battery Connector | | Lights - Head and Tail |
| | Battery - Discharge Indicator | | Lights - Warning |
| | Belt | | Mast |
| | Brakes - Parking | | Oil Leaks |
| | Brakes - Service | | Oil Pressure |
| | Cables | | Overhead Guard |
| | Engine Oil Level | | Radiator Level |
| | Forks | | Safety Equipment |
| | Fuel | | Steering |
| | Gauges | | Tires |
| | Horn | | Unusual Noises |
| | Hoses | | Other _____ |

Notes: _____
_____
_____
_____
_____
_____
_____
_____
_____

Operator's Name: _____

Operator's Signature: _____

Supervisor's Name: _____

Supervisor's Signature: _____

Date: _____ Shift: _____

Truck Number:_____ Electric:____ Internal Combustion:____

Hour Meter Start:_____ End:_____ Total Hours:_____

Check any defective item and explain in the notes section below:

| | | | |
|---|---|---|---|
| | Accelerator | | Hour Meter |
| | Alarms | | Hydraulic Controls |
| | Battery Connector | | Lights - Head and Tail |
| | Battery - Discharge Indicator | | Lights - Warning |
| | Belt | | Mast |
| | Brakes - Parking | | Oil Leaks |
| | Brakes - Service | | Oil Pressure |
| | Cables | | Overhead Guard |
| | Engine Oil Level | | Radiator Level |
| | Forks | | Safety Equipment |
| | Fuel | | Steering |
| | Gauges | | Tires |
| | Horn | | Unusual Noises |
| | Hoses | | Other _____ |

Notes:_____

_____

_____

_____

_____

_____

_____

_____

_____

Operator's Name:_____

Operator's Signature:_____

Supervisor's Name:_____

Supervisor's Signature:_____

Date: _____ Shift: _____

Truck Number:_____ Electric:___ Internal Combustion:___

Hour Meter Start:_____ End:_____ Total Hours:_____

Check any defective item and explain in the notes section below:

| | | | |
|---|---|---|---|
| | Accelerator | | Hour Meter |
| | Alarms | | Hydraulic Controls |
| | Battery Connector | | Lights - Head and Tail |
| | Battery - Discharge Indicator | | Lights - Warning |
| | Belt | | Mast |
| | Brakes - Parking | | Oil Leaks |
| | Brakes - Service | | Oil Pressure |
| | Cables | | Overhead Guard |
| | Engine Oil Level | | Radiator Level |
| | Forks | | Safety Equipment |
| | Fuel | | Steering |
| | Gauges | | Tires |
| | Horn | | Unusual Noises |
| | Hoses | | Other _____ |

Notes:_____

_____

_____

_____

_____

_____

_____

_____

_____

Operator's Name:_____

Operator's Signature:_____

Supervisor's Name:_____

Supervisor's Signature:_____

Date: _____ Shift: _____

Truck Number:_____ Electric:___ Internal Combustion:___

Hour Meter Start:_____ End:_____ Total Hours:_____

Check any defective item and explain in the notes section below:

| | Accelerator | | Hour Meter |
|---|---|---|---|
| | Alarms | | Hydraulic Controls |
| | Battery Connector | | Lights - Head and Tail |
| | Battery - Discharge Indicator | | Lights - Warning |
| | Belt | | Mast |
| | Brakes - Parking | | Oil Leaks |
| | Brakes - Service | | Oil Pressure |
| | Cables | | Overhead Guard |
| | Engine Oil Level | | Radiator Level |
| | Forks | | Safety Equipment |
| | Fuel | | Steering |
| | Gauges | | Tires |
| | Horn | | Unusual Noises |
| | Hoses | | Other _____ |

Notes:_____

_____

_____

_____

_____

_____

_____

_____

_____

Operator's Name:_____

Operator's Signature:_____

Supervisor's Name:_____

Supervisor's Signature:_____

Date: _____ Shift: _____

Truck Number:_____ Electric:____ Internal Combustion:____

Hour Meter Start:_____ End:_____ Total Hours:_____

Check any defective item and explain in the notes section below:

| | | | |
|---|---|---|---|
| | Accelerator | | Hour Meter |
| | Alarms | | Hydraulic Controls |
| | Battery Connector | | Lights - Head and Tail |
| | Battery - Discharge Indicator | | Lights - Warning |
| | Belt | | Mast |
| | Brakes - Parking | | Oil Leaks |
| | Brakes - Service | | Oil Pressure |
| | Cables | | Overhead Guard |
| | Engine Oil Level | | Radiator Level |
| | Forks | | Safety Equipment |
| | Fuel | | Steering |
| | Gauges | | Tires |
| | Horn | | Unusual Noises |
| | Hoses | | Other _____ |

Notes:_____

_____

_____

_____

_____

_____

_____

_____

_____

Operator's Name:_____

Operator's Signature:_____

Supervisor's Name:_____

Supervisor's Signature:_____

Date: _____ Shift: _____

Truck Number:_____ Electric:____ Internal Combustion:____

Hour Meter Start:_____ End:_____ Total Hours:_____

Check any defective item and explain in the notes section below:

| | | | |
|---|---|---|---|
| | Accelerator | | Hour Meter |
| | Alarms | | Hydraulic Controls |
| | Battery Connector | | Lights - Head and Tail |
| | Battery - Discharge Indicator | | Lights - Warning |
| | Belt | | Mast |
| | Brakes - Parking | | Oil Leaks |
| | Brakes - Service | | Oil Pressure |
| | Cables | | Overhead Guard |
| | Engine Oil Level | | Radiator Level |
| | Forks | | Safety Equipment |
| | Fuel | | Steering |
| | Gauges | | Tires |
| | Horn | | Unusual Noises |
| | Hoses | | Other _____ |

Notes:_____

_____

_____

_____

_____

_____

_____

_____

_____

_____

Operator's Name:_____

Operator's Signature:_____

Supervisor's Name:_____

Supervisor's Signature:_____

Date: _____ Shift: _____

Truck Number:_____ Electric:____ Internal Combustion:____

Hour Meter Start:_____ End:_____ Total Hours:_____

Check any defective item and explain in the notes section below:

| | | | |
|---|---|---|---|
| | Accelerator | | Hour Meter |
| | Alarms | | Hydraulic Controls |
| | Battery Connector | | Lights - Head and Tail |
| | Battery - Discharge Indicator | | Lights - Warning |
| | Belt | | Mast |
| | Brakes - Parking | | Oil Leaks |
| | Brakes - Service | | Oil Pressure |
| | Cables | | Overhead Guard |
| | Engine Oil Level | | Radiator Level |
| | Forks | | Safety Equipment |
| | Fuel | | Steering |
| | Gauges | | Tires |
| | Horn | | Unusual Noises |
| | Hoses | | Other _____ |

Notes:_____

_____

_____

_____

_____

_____

_____

_____

_____

Operator's Name:_____

Operator's Signature:_____

Supervisor's Name:_____

Supervisor's Signature:_____

Date: _____ Shift: _____

Truck Number: _____ Electric: ____ Internal Combustion: ____

Hour Meter Start: _____ End: _____ Total Hours: _____

Check any defective item and explain in the notes section below:

| | | | |
|---|---|---|---|
| | Accelerator | | Hour Meter |
| | Alarms | | Hydraulic Controls |
| | Battery Connector | | Lights - Head and Tail |
| | Battery - Discharge Indicator | | Lights - Warning |
| | Belt | | Mast |
| | Brakes - Parking | | Oil Leaks |
| | Brakes - Service | | Oil Pressure |
| | Cables | | Overhead Guard |
| | Engine Oil Level | | Radiator Level |
| | Forks | | Safety Equipment |
| | Fuel | | Steering |
| | Gauges | | Tires |
| | Horn | | Unusual Noises |
| | Hoses | | Other _____ |

Notes: _____
_____
_____
_____
_____
_____
_____
_____
_____

Operator's Name: _____

Operator's Signature: _____

Supervisor's Name: _____

Supervisor's Signature: _____

Date: _____  Shift: _____

Truck Number: _____  Electric: ____  Internal Combustion: ____

Hour Meter Start: _____ End: _____ Total Hours: _____

Check any defective item and explain in the notes section below:

| | | | |
|---|---|---|---|
| | Accelerator | | Hour Meter |
| | Alarms | | Hydraulic Controls |
| | Battery Connector | | Lights - Head and Tail |
| | Battery - Discharge Indicator | | Lights - Warning |
| | Belt | | Mast |
| | Brakes - Parking | | Oil Leaks |
| | Brakes - Service | | Oil Pressure |
| | Cables | | Overhead Guard |
| | Engine Oil Level | | Radiator Level |
| | Forks | | Safety Equipment |
| | Fuel | | Steering |
| | Gauges | | Tires |
| | Horn | | Unusual Noises |
| | Hoses | | Other _____ |

Notes:_____.
_____
_____
_____
_____
_____
_____
_____
_____

Operator's Name:_____

Operator's Signature:_____

Supervisor's Name:_____

Supervisor's Signature:_____

Date: _____ Shift: _____

Truck Number:_____ Electric:___ Internal Combustion:___

Hour Meter Start:_____ End:_____ Total Hours:_____

Check any defective item and explain in the notes section below:

| | | | |
|---|---|---|---|
| | Accelerator | | Hour Meter |
| | Alarms | | Hydraulic Controls |
| | Battery Connector | | Lights - Head and Tail |
| | Battery - Discharge Indicator | | Lights - Warning |
| | Belt | | Mast |
| | Brakes - Parking | | Oil Leaks |
| | Brakes - Service | | Oil Pressure |
| | Cables | | Overhead Guard |
| | Engine Oil Level | | Radiator Level |
| | Forks | | Safety Equipment |
| | Fuel | | Steering |
| | Gauges | | Tires |
| | Horn | | Unusual Noises |
| | Hoses | | Other _____ |

Notes:_____

_____

_____

_____

_____

_____

_____

_____

_____

Operator's Name:_____

Operator's Signature:_____

Supervisor's Name:_____

Supervisor's Signature:_____

Date: _____ Shift: _____

Truck Number:_____ Electric:____ Internal Combustion:____

Hour Meter Start:_____ End:_____ Total Hours:_____

Check any defective item and explain in the notes section below:

| |  | |  |
|---|---|---|---|
| | Accelerator | | Hour Meter |
| | Alarms | | Hydraulic Controls |
| | Battery Connector | | Lights - Head and Tail |
| | Battery - Discharge Indicator | | Lights - Warning |
| | Belt | | Mast |
| | Brakes - Parking | | Oil Leaks |
| | Brakes - Service | | Oil Pressure |
| | Cables | | Overhead Guard |
| | Engine Oil Level | | Radiator Level |
| | Forks | | Safety Equipment |
| | Fuel | | Steering |
| | Gauges | | Tires |
| | Horn | | Unusual Noises |
| | Hoses | | Other _____ |

Notes:_____

_____

_____

_____

_____

_____

_____

_____

_____

Operator's Name:_____

Operator's Signature:_____

Supervisor's Name:_____

Supervisor's Signature:_____

Date: _____ Shift: _____

Truck Number:_____ Electric:____ Internal Combustion:____

Hour Meter Start:_____ End:_____ Total Hours:_____

Check any defective item and explain in the notes section below:

| | | | |
|---|---|---|---|
| | Accelerator | | Hour Meter |
| | Alarms | | Hydraulic Controls |
| | Battery Connector | | Lights - Head and Tail |
| | Battery - Discharge Indicator | | Lights - Warning |
| | Belt | | Mast |
| | Brakes - Parking | | Oil Leaks |
| | Brakes - Service | | Oil Pressure |
| | Cables | | Overhead Guard |
| | Engine Oil Level | | Radiator Level |
| | Forks | | Safety Equipment |
| | Fuel | | Steering |
| | Gauges | | Tires |
| | Horn | | Unusual Noises |
| | Hoses | | Other _____ |

Notes:_____
_____
_____
_____
_____
_____
_____
_____
_____

Operator's Name:_____

Operator's Signature:_____

Supervisor's Name:_____

Supervisor's Signature:_____

Date: _____ Shift: _____

Truck Number:_____ Electric:____ Internal Combustion:____

Hour Meter Start:_____ End:_____ Total Hours:_____

Check any defective item and explain in the notes section below:

| | | | |
|---|---|---|---|
| | Accelerator | | Hour Meter |
| | Alarms | | Hydraulic Controls |
| | Battery Connector | | Lights - Head and Tail |
| | Battery - Discharge Indicator | | Lights - Warning |
| | Belt | | Mast |
| | Brakes - Parking | | Oil Leaks |
| | Brakes - Service | | Oil Pressure |
| | Cables | | Overhead Guard |
| | Engine Oil Level | | Radiator Level |
| | Forks | | Safety Equipment |
| | Fuel | | Steering |
| | Gauges | | Tires |
| | Horn | | Unusual Noises |
| | Hoses | | Other _____ |

Notes:_____

_____

_____

_____

_____

_____

_____

_____

_____

Operator's Name:_____

Operator's Signature:_____

Supervisor's Name:_____

Supervisor's Signature:_____

Date: _____ Shift: _____

Truck Number:_____ Electric:____ Internal Combustion:____

Hour Meter Start:_____ End:_____ Total Hours:_____

Check any defective item and explain in the notes section below:

| | | | |
|---|---|---|---|
| | Accelerator | | Hour Meter |
| | Alarms | | Hydraulic Controls |
| | Battery Connector | | Lights - Head and Tail |
| | Battery - Discharge Indicator | | Lights - Warning |
| | Belt | | Mast |
| | Brakes - Parking | | Oil Leaks |
| | Brakes - Service | | Oil Pressure |
| | Cables | | Overhead Guard |
| | Engine Oil Level | | Radiator Level |
| | Forks | | Safety Equipment |
| | Fuel | | Steering |
| | Gauges | | Tires |
| | Horn | | Unusual Noises |
| | Hoses | | Other _____ |

Notes:_____

_____

_____

_____

_____

_____

_____

_____

_____

Operator's Name:_____

Operator's Signature:_____

Supervisor's Name:_____

Supervisor's Signature:_____

Date: _____ Shift: _____

Truck Number:_____ Electric:____ Internal Combustion:____

Hour Meter Start:_____ End:_____ Total Hours:_____

Check any defective item and explain in the notes section below:

| | | | |
|---|---|---|---|
| | Accelerator | | Hour Meter |
| | Alarms | | Hydraulic Controls |
| | Battery Connector | | Lights - Head and Tail |
| | Battery - Discharge Indicator | | Lights - Warning |
| | Belt | | Mast |
| | Brakes - Parking | | Oil Leaks |
| | Brakes - Service | | Oil Pressure |
| | Cables | | Overhead Guard |
| | Engine Oil Level | | Radiator Level |
| | Forks | | Safety Equipment |
| | Fuel | | Steering |
| | Gauges | | Tires |
| | Horn | | Unusual Noises |
| | Hoses | | Other _____ |

Notes:_____

_____

_____

_____

_____

_____

_____

_____

_____

Operator's Name:_____

Operator's Signature:_____

Supervisor's Name:_____

Supervisor's Signature:_____

Date: _____    Shift: _____

Truck Number: _____    Electric: ____    Internal Combustion: ____

Hour Meter Start: _____ End: _____ Total Hours: _____

Check any defective item and explain in the notes section below:

| | | | |
|---|---|---|---|
| | Accelerator | | Hour Meter |
| | Alarms | | Hydraulic Controls |
| | Battery Connector | | Lights - Head and Tail |
| | Battery - Discharge Indicator | | Lights - Warning |
| | Belt | | Mast |
| | Brakes - Parking | | Oil Leaks |
| | Brakes - Service | | Oil Pressure |
| | Cables | | Overhead Guard |
| | Engine Oil Level | | Radiator Level |
| | Forks | | Safety Equipment |
| | Fuel | | Steering |
| | Gauges | | Tires |
| | Horn | | Unusual Noises |
| | Hoses | | Other _____ |

Notes: _____

_____

_____

_____

_____

_____

_____

_____

_____

Operator's Name: _____

Operator's Signature: _____

Supervisor's Name: _____

Supervisor's Signature: _____

Date: _____   Shift: _____

Truck Number:_____   Electric:____  Internal Combustion:____

Hour Meter Start:_____  End:_____  Total Hours:_____

Check any defective item and explain in the notes section below:

|  |  |  |  |
|---|---|---|---|
|  | Accelerator |  | Hour Meter |
|  | Alarms |  | Hydraulic Controls |
|  | Battery Connector |  | Lights - Head and Tail |
|  | Battery - Discharge Indicator |  | Lights - Warning |
|  | Belt |  | Mast |
|  | Brakes - Parking |  | Oil Leaks |
|  | Brakes - Service |  | Oil Pressure |
|  | Cables |  | Overhead Guard |
|  | Engine Oil Level |  | Radiator Level |
|  | Forks |  | Safety Equipment |
|  | Fuel |  | Steering |
|  | Gauges |  | Tires |
|  | Horn |  | Unusual Noises |
|  | Hoses |  | Other _____ |

Notes:_____
_____
_____
_____
_____
_____
_____
_____
_____

Operator's Name:_____

Operator's Signature:_____

Supervisor's Name:_____

Supervisor's Signature:_____

Date: _____ Shift: _____

Truck Number:_____ Electric:___ Internal Combustion:___

Hour Meter Start:_____ End:_____ Total Hours:_____

Check any defective item and explain in the notes section below:

| | | | |
|---|---|---|---|
| | Accelerator | | Hour Meter |
| | Alarms | | Hydraulic Controls |
| | Battery Connector | | Lights - Head and Tail |
| | Battery - Discharge Indicator | | Lights - Warning |
| | Belt | | Mast |
| | Brakes - Parking | | Oil Leaks |
| | Brakes - Service | | Oil Pressure |
| | Cables | | Overhead Guard |
| | Engine Oil Level | | Radiator Level |
| | Forks | | Safety Equipment |
| | Fuel | | Steering |
| | Gauges | | Tires |
| | Horn | | Unusual Noises |
| | Hoses | | Other _____ |

Notes:_____

_____

_____

_____

_____

_____

_____

_____

_____

_____

Operator's Name:_____

Operator's Signature:_____

Supervisor's Name:_____

Supervisor's Signature:_____

Date: _____  Shift: _____

Truck Number: _____  Electric: ____  Internal Combustion: ____

Hour Meter Start: _____ End: _____ Total Hours: _____

Check any defective item and explain in the notes section below:

| | | | |
|---|---|---|---|
| | Accelerator | | Hour Meter |
| | Alarms | | Hydraulic Controls |
| | Battery Connector | | Lights - Head and Tail |
| | Battery - Discharge Indicator | | Lights - Warning |
| | Belt | | Mast |
| | Brakes - Parking | | Oil Leaks |
| | Brakes - Service | | Oil Pressure |
| | Cables | | Overhead Guard |
| | Engine Oil Level | | Radiator Level |
| | Forks | | Safety Equipment |
| | Fuel | | Steering |
| | Gauges | | Tires |
| | Horn | | Unusual Noises |
| | Hoses | | Other _____ |

Notes: _____

_____

_____

_____

_____

_____

_____

_____

_____

Operator's Name: _____

Operator's Signature: _____

Supervisor's Name: _____

Supervisor's Signature: _____

Date: _____ Shift: _____

Truck Number:_____ Electric:____ Internal Combustion:____

Hour Meter Start:_____ End:_____ Total Hours:_____

Check any defective item and explain in the notes section below:

| | | | |
|---|---|---|---|
| | Accelerator | | Hour Meter |
| | Alarms | | Hydraulic Controls |
| | Battery Connector | | Lights - Head and Tail |
| | Battery - Discharge Indicator | | Lights - Warning |
| | Belt | | Mast |
| | Brakes - Parking | | Oil Leaks |
| | Brakes - Service | | Oil Pressure |
| | Cables | | Overhead Guard |
| | Engine Oil Level | | Radiator Level |
| | Forks | | Safety Equipment |
| | Fuel | | Steering |
| | Gauges | | Tires |
| | Horn | | Unusual Noises |
| | Hoses | | Other _____ |

Notes:_____

_____

_____

_____

_____

_____

_____

_____

_____

Operator's Name:_____

Operator's Signature:_____

Supervisor's Name:_____

Supervisor's Signature:_____

Date: _____ Shift: _____

Truck Number:_____ Electric:____ Internal Combustion:____

Hour Meter Start:_____ End:_____ Total Hours:_____

Check any defective item and explain in the notes section below:

| | | | |
|---|---|---|---|
| | Accelerator | | Hour Meter |
| | Alarms | | Hydraulic Controls |
| | Battery Connector | | Lights - Head and Tail |
| | Battery - Discharge Indicator | | Lights - Warning |
| | Belt | | Mast |
| | Brakes - Parking | | Oil Leaks |
| | Brakes - Service | | Oil Pressure |
| | Cables | | Overhead Guard |
| | Engine Oil Level | | Radiator Level |
| | Forks | | Safety Equipment |
| | Fuel | | Steering |
| | Gauges | | Tires |
| | Horn | | Unusual Noises |
| | Hoses | | Other _____ |

Notes:_____

_____

_____

_____

_____

_____

_____

_____

_____

Operator's Name:_____

Operator's Signature:_____

Supervisor's Name:_____

Supervisor's Signature:_____

Date: _____ Shift: _____

Truck Number:_____ Electric:____ Internal Combustion:____

Hour Meter Start:_____ End:_____ Total Hours:_____

Check any defective item and explain in the notes section below:

| | | | |
|---|---|---|---|
| | Accelerator | | Hour Meter |
| | Alarms | | Hydraulic Controls |
| | Battery Connector | | Lights - Head and Tail |
| | Battery - Discharge Indicator | | Lights - Warning |
| | Belt | | Mast |
| | Brakes - Parking | | Oil Leaks |
| | Brakes - Service | | Oil Pressure |
| | Cables | | Overhead Guard |
| | Engine Oil Level | | Radiator Level |
| | Forks | | Safety Equipment |
| | Fuel | | Steering |
| | Gauges | | Tires |
| | Horn | | Unusual Noises |
| | Hoses | | Other _____ |

Notes:_____

_____

_____

_____

_____

_____

_____

_____

_____

Operator's Name:_____

Operator's Signature:_____

Supervisor's Name:_____

Supervisor's Signature:_____

Date: _____ Shift: _____

Truck Number:_____ Electric:___ Internal Combustion:___

Hour Meter Start:_____ End:_____ Total Hours:_____

Check any defective item and explain in the notes section below:

| | | | |
|---|---|---|---|
| | Accelerator | | Hour Meter |
| | Alarms | | Hydraulic Controls |
| | Battery Connector | | Lights - Head and Tail |
| | Battery - Discharge Indicator | | Lights - Warning |
| | Belt | | Mast |
| | Brakes - Parking | | Oil Leaks |
| | Brakes - Service | | Oil Pressure |
| | Cables | | Overhead Guard |
| | Engine Oil Level | | Radiator Level |
| | Forks | | Safety Equipment |
| | Fuel | | Steering |
| | Gauges | | Tires |
| | Horn | | Unusual Noises |
| | Hoses | | Other _____ |

Notes:_____
_____
_____
_____
_____
_____
_____
_____
_____

Operator's Name:_____

Operator's Signature:_____

Supervisor's Name:_____

Supervisor's Signature:_____

Date: _____ Shift: _____

Truck Number:_____ Electric:___ Internal Combustion:___

Hour Meter Start:_____ End:_____ Total Hours:_____

Check any defective item and explain in the notes section below:

| | | | |
|---|---|---|---|
| | Accelerator | | Hour Meter |
| | Alarms | | Hydraulic Controls |
| | Battery Connector | | Lights - Head and Tail |
| | Battery - Discharge Indicator | | Lights - Warning |
| | Belt | | Mast |
| | Brakes - Parking | | Oil Leaks |
| | Brakes - Service | | Oil Pressure |
| | Cables | | Overhead Guard |
| | Engine Oil Level | | Radiator Level |
| | Forks | | Safety Equipment |
| | Fuel | | Steering |
| | Gauges | | Tires |
| | Horn | | Unusual Noises |
| | Hoses | | Other _____ |

Notes:_____

_____

_____

_____

_____

_____

_____

_____

_____

Operator's Name:_____

Operator's Signature:_____

Supervisor's Name:_____

Supervisor's Signature:_____

Date: _____ Shift: _____

Truck Number:_____ Electric:____ Internal Combustion:____

Hour Meter Start:_____ End:_____ Total Hours:_____

Check any defective item and explain in the notes section below:

| | | | |
|---|---|---|---|
| | Accelerator | | Hour Meter |
| | Alarms | | Hydraulic Controls |
| | Battery Connector | | Lights - Head and Tail |
| | Battery - Discharge Indicator | | Lights - Warning |
| | Belt | | Mast |
| | Brakes - Parking | | Oil Leaks |
| | Brakes - Service | | Oil Pressure |
| | Cables | | Overhead Guard |
| | Engine Oil Level | | Radiator Level |
| | Forks | | Safety Equipment |
| | Fuel | | Steering |
| | Gauges | | Tires |
| | Horn | | Unusual Noises |
| | Hoses | | Other _____ |

Notes:_____

_____

_____

_____

_____

_____

_____

_____

_____

Operator's Name:_____

Operator's Signature:_____

Supervisor's Name:_____

Supervisor's Signature:_____

Date: _____ Shift: _____

Truck Number:_____ Electric:____ Internal Combustion:____

Hour Meter Start:_____ End:_____ Total Hours:_____

Check any defective item and explain in the notes section below:

| | | | |
|---|---|---|---|
| | Accelerator | | Hour Meter |
| | Alarms | | Hydraulic Controls |
| | Battery Connector | | Lights - Head and Tail |
| | Battery - Discharge Indicator | | Lights - Warning |
| | Belt | | Mast |
| | Brakes - Parking | | Oil Leaks |
| | Brakes - Service | | Oil Pressure |
| | Cables | | Overhead Guard |
| | Engine Oil Level | | Radiator Level |
| | Forks | | Safety Equipment |
| | Fuel | | Steering |
| | Gauges | | Tires |
| | Horn | | Unusual Noises |
| | Hoses | | Other _____ |

Notes:_____

_____

_____

_____

_____

_____

_____

_____

_____

Operator's Name:_____

Operator's Signature:_____

Supervisor's Name:_____

Supervisor's Signature:_____

Date: _____ Shift: _____

Truck Number:_____ Electric:____ Internal Combustion:____

Hour Meter Start:_____ End:_____ Total Hours:_____

Check any defective item and explain in the notes section below:

| | | | |
|---|---|---|---|
| | Accelerator | | Hour Meter |
| | Alarms | | Hydraulic Controls |
| | Battery Connector | | Lights - Head and Tail |
| | Battery - Discharge Indicator | | Lights - Warning |
| | Belt | | Mast |
| | Brakes - Parking | | Oil Leaks |
| | Brakes - Service | | Oil Pressure |
| | Cables | | Overhead Guard |
| | Engine Oil Level | | Radiator Level |
| | Forks | | Safety Equipment |
| | Fuel | | Steering |
| | Gauges | | Tires |
| | Horn | | Unusual Noises |
| | Hoses | | Other _____ |

Notes:_____

_____

_____

_____

_____

_____

_____

_____

Operator's Name:_____

Operator's Signature:_____

Supervisor's Name:_____

Supervisor's Signature:_____

Date: _____ Shift: _____

Truck Number:_____ Electric:____ Internal Combustion:____

Hour Meter Start:_____ End:_____ Total Hours:_____

Check any defective item and explain in the notes section below:

| | | | |
|---|---|---|---|
| | Accelerator | | Hour Meter |
| | Alarms | | Hydraulic Controls |
| | Battery Connector | | Lights - Head and Tail |
| | Battery - Discharge Indicator | | Lights - Warning |
| | Belt | | Mast |
| | Brakes - Parking | | Oil Leaks |
| | Brakes - Service | | Oil Pressure |
| | Cables | | Overhead Guard |
| | Engine Oil Level | | Radiator Level |
| | Forks | | Safety Equipment |
| | Fuel | | Steering |
| | Gauges | | Tires |
| | Horn | | Unusual Noises |
| | Hoses | | Other _____ |

Notes:_____
_____
_____
_____
_____
_____
_____
_____
_____
_____

Operator's Name:_____

Operator's Signature:_____

Supervisor's Name:_____

Supervisor's Signature:_____

Date: _____ Shift: _____

Truck Number:_____ Electric:____ Internal Combustion:____

Hour Meter Start:_____ End:_____ Total Hours:_____

Check any defective item and explain in the notes section below:

| | | | |
|---|---|---|---|
| | Accelerator | | Hour Meter |
| | Alarms | | Hydraulic Controls |
| | Battery Connector | | Lights - Head and Tail |
| | Battery - Discharge Indicator | | Lights - Warning |
| | Belt | | Mast |
| | Brakes - Parking | | Oil Leaks |
| | Brakes - Service | | Oil Pressure |
| | Cables | | Overhead Guard |
| | Engine Oil Level | | Radiator Level |
| | Forks | | Safety Equipment |
| | Fuel | | Steering |
| | Gauges | | Tires |
| | Horn | | Unusual Noises |
| | Hoses | | Other _____ |

Notes:_____

_____

_____

_____

_____

_____

_____

_____

_____

Operator's Name:_____

Operator's Signature:_____

Supervisor's Name:_____

Supervisor's Signature:_____

Date: _____ Shift: _____

Truck Number:_____ Electric:___ Internal Combustion:___

Hour Meter Start:_____ End:_____ Total Hours:_____

Check any defective item and explain in the notes section below:

| | | | |
|---|---|---|---|
| | Accelerator | | Hour Meter |
| | Alarms | | Hydraulic Controls |
| | Battery Connector | | Lights - Head and Tail |
| | Battery - Discharge Indicator | | Lights - Warning |
| | Belt | | Mast |
| | Brakes - Parking | | Oil Leaks |
| | Brakes - Service | | Oil Pressure |
| | Cables | | Overhead Guard |
| | Engine Oil Level | | Radiator Level |
| | Forks | | Safety Equipment |
| | Fuel | | Steering |
| | Gauges | | Tires |
| | Horn | | Unusual Noises |
| | Hoses | | Other _____ |

Notes:_____

_____

_____

_____

_____

_____

_____

_____

_____

Operator's Name:_____

Operator's Signature:_____

Supervisor's Name:_____

Supervisor's Signature:_____

Date: _____ Shift: _____

Truck Number: _____ Electric: ___ Internal Combustion: ___

Hour Meter Start: _____ End: _____ Total Hours: _____

Check any defective item and explain in the notes section below:

| | | | |
|---|---|---|---|
| | Accelerator | | Hour Meter |
| | Alarms | | Hydraulic Controls |
| | Battery Connector | | Lights - Head and Tail |
| | Battery - Discharge Indicator | | Lights - Warning |
| | Belt | | Mast |
| | Brakes - Parking | | Oil Leaks |
| | Brakes - Service | | Oil Pressure |
| | Cables | | Overhead Guard |
| | Engine Oil Level | | Radiator Level |
| | Forks | | Safety Equipment |
| | Fuel | | Steering |
| | Gauges | | Tires |
| | Horn | | Unusual Noises |
| | Hoses | | Other _____ |

Notes: _____

_____

_____

_____

_____

_____

_____

_____

_____

Operator's Name: _____

Operator's Signature: _____

Supervisor's Name: _____

Supervisor's Signature: _____

Date: _____ Shift: _____

Truck Number:_____ Electric:___ Internal Combustion:___

Hour Meter Start:_____ End:_____ Total Hours:_____

Check any defective item and explain in the notes section below:

| | | | |
|---|---|---|---|
| | Accelerator | | Hour Meter |
| | Alarms | | Hydraulic Controls |
| | Battery Connector | | Lights - Head and Tail |
| | Battery - Discharge Indicator | | Lights - Warning |
| | Belt | | Mast |
| | Brakes - Parking | | Oil Leaks |
| | Brakes - Service | | Oil Pressure |
| | Cables | | Overhead Guard |
| | Engine Oil Level | | Radiator Level |
| | Forks | | Safety Equipment |
| | Fuel | | Steering |
| | Gauges | | Tires |
| | Horn | | Unusual Noises |
| | Hoses | | Other _____ |

Notes:_____
_____
_____
_____
_____
_____
_____
_____
_____

Operator's Name:_____

Operator's Signature:_____

Supervisor's Name:_____

Supervisor's Signature:_____

Date: _____ Shift: _____

Truck Number:_____ Electric:____ Internal Combustion:____

Hour Meter Start:_____ End:_____ Total Hours:_____

Check any defective item and explain in the notes section below:

| | | | |
|---|---|---|---|
| | Accelerator | | Hour Meter |
| | Alarms | | Hydraulic Controls |
| | Battery Connector | | Lights - Head and Tail |
| | Battery - Discharge Indicator | | Lights - Warning |
| | Belt | | Mast |
| | Brakes - Parking | | Oil Leaks |
| | Brakes - Service | | Oil Pressure |
| | Cables | | Overhead Guard |
| | Engine Oil Level | | Radiator Level |
| | Forks | | Safety Equipment |
| | Fuel | | Steering |
| | Gauges | | Tires |
| | Horn | | Unusual Noises |
| | Hoses | | Other _____ |

Notes:_____

_____

_____

_____

_____

_____

_____

_____

_____

Operator's Name:_____

Operator's Signature:_____

Supervisor's Name:_____

Supervisor's Signature:_____

Date: _____ Shift: _____

Truck Number: _____ Electric: ____ Internal Combustion: ____

Hour Meter Start: _____ End: _____ Total Hours: _____

Check any defective item and explain in the notes section below:

| | | | |
|---|---|---|---|
| | Accelerator | | Hour Meter |
| | Alarms | | Hydraulic Controls |
| | Battery Connector | | Lights - Head and Tail |
| | Battery - Discharge Indicator | | Lights - Warning |
| | Belt | | Mast |
| | Brakes - Parking | | Oil Leaks |
| | Brakes - Service | | Oil Pressure |
| | Cables | | Overhead Guard |
| | Engine Oil Level | | Radiator Level |
| | Forks | | Safety Equipment |
| | Fuel | | Steering |
| | Gauges | | Tires |
| | Horn | | Unusual Noises |
| | Hoses | | Other _____ |

Notes:_____
_____
_____
_____
_____
_____
_____
_____
_____

Operator's Name:_____

Operator's Signature:_____

Supervisor's Name:_____

Supervisor's Signature:_____

Date: _____ Shift: _____

Truck Number:_____ Electric:____ Internal Combustion:____

Hour Meter Start:_____ End:_____ Total Hours:_____

Check any defective item and explain in the notes section below:

| | | | |
|---|---|---|---|
| | Accelerator | | Hour Meter |
| | Alarms | | Hydraulic Controls |
| | Battery Connector | | Lights - Head and Tail |
| | Battery - Discharge Indicator | | Lights - Warning |
| | Belt | | Mast |
| | Brakes - Parking | | Oil Leaks |
| | Brakes - Service | | Oil Pressure |
| | Cables | | Overhead Guard |
| | Engine Oil Level | | Radiator Level |
| | Forks | | Safety Equipment |
| | Fuel | | Steering |
| | Gauges | | Tires |
| | Horn | | Unusual Noises |
| | Hoses | | Other _____ |

Notes:_____

_____

_____

_____

_____

_____

_____

_____

_____

_____

Operator's Name:_____

Operator's Signature:_____

Supervisor's Name:_____

Supervisor's Signature:_____

Date: _____ Shift: _____

Truck Number: _____ Electric: ____ Internal Combustion: ____

Hour Meter Start: _____ End: _____ Total Hours: _____

Check any defective item and explain in the notes section below:

| | | | |
|---|---|---|---|
| | Accelerator | | Hour Meter |
| | Alarms | | Hydraulic Controls |
| | Battery Connector | | Lights - Head and Tail |
| | Battery - Discharge Indicator | | Lights - Warning |
| | Belt | | Mast |
| | Brakes - Parking | | Oil Leaks |
| | Brakes - Service | | Oil Pressure |
| | Cables | | Overhead Guard |
| | Engine Oil Level | | Radiator Level |
| | Forks | | Safety Equipment |
| | Fuel | | Steering |
| | Gauges | | Tires |
| | Horn | | Unusual Noises |
| | Hoses | | Other _____ |

Notes: _____

_____

_____

_____

_____

_____

_____

_____

_____

Operator's Name: _____

Operator's Signature: _____

Supervisor's Name: _____

Supervisor's Signature: _____

Date: _____ Shift: _____

Truck Number:_____ Electric:____ Internal Combustion:____

Hour Meter Start:_____ End:_____ Total Hours:_____

Check any defective item and explain in the notes section below:

| | | | |
|---|---|---|---|
| | Accelerator | | Hour Meter |
| | Alarms | | Hydraulic Controls |
| | Battery Connector | | Lights - Head and Tail |
| | Battery - Discharge Indicator | | Lights - Warning |
| | Belt | | Mast |
| | Brakes - Parking | | Oil Leaks |
| | Brakes - Service | | Oil Pressure |
| | Cables | | Overhead Guard |
| | Engine Oil Level | | Radiator Level |
| | Forks | | Safety Equipment |
| | Fuel | | Steering |
| | Gauges | | Tires |
| | Horn | | Unusual Noises |
| | Hoses | | Other _____ |

Notes:_____

_____

_____

_____

_____

_____

_____

_____

_____

Operator's Name:_____

Operator's Signature:_____

Supervisor's Name:_____

Supervisor's Signature:_____

Date: _____ Shift: _____

Truck Number:_____ Electric:____ Internal Combustion:____

Hour Meter Start:_____ End:_____ Total Hours:_____

Check any defective item and explain in the notes section below:

| | | | |
|---|---|---|---|
| | Accelerator | | Hour Meter |
| | Alarms | | Hydraulic Controls |
| | Battery Connector | | Lights - Head and Tail |
| | Battery - Discharge Indicator | | Lights - Warning |
| | Belt | | Mast |
| | Brakes - Parking | | Oil Leaks |
| | Brakes - Service | | Oil Pressure |
| | Cables | | Overhead Guard |
| | Engine Oil Level | | Radiator Level |
| | Forks | | Safety Equipment |
| | Fuel | | Steering |
| | Gauges | | Tires |
| | Horn | | Unusual Noises |
| | Hoses | | Other _____ |

Notes:_____

_____

_____

_____

_____

_____

_____

_____

_____

Operator's Name:_____

Operator's Signature:_____

Supervisor's Name:_____

Supervisor's Signature:_____

Date: _____ Shift: _____

Truck Number:_____ Electric:___ Internal Combustion:___

Hour Meter Start:_____ End:_____ Total Hours:_____

Check any defective item and explain in the notes section below:

| | | | |
|---|---|---|---|
| | Accelerator | | Hour Meter |
| | Alarms | | Hydraulic Controls |
| | Battery Connector | | Lights - Head and Tail |
| | Battery - Discharge Indicator | | Lights - Warning |
| | Belt | | Mast |
| | Brakes - Parking | | Oil Leaks |
| | Brakes - Service | | Oil Pressure |
| | Cables | | Overhead Guard |
| | Engine Oil Level | | Radiator Level |
| | Forks | | Safety Equipment |
| | Fuel | | Steering |
| | Gauges | | Tires |
| | Horn | | Unusual Noises |
| | Hoses | | Other _____ |

Notes:_____
_____
_____
_____
_____
_____
_____
_____
_____

Operator's Name:_____

Operator's Signature:_____

Supervisor's Name:_____

Supervisor's Signature:_____

Date: _____  Shift: _____

Truck Number:_____  Electric:____  Internal Combustion:____

Hour Meter Start:_____ End:_____ Total Hours:_____

Check any defective item and explain in the notes section below:

| | | | |
|---|---|---|---|
| | Accelerator | | Hour Meter |
| | Alarms | | Hydraulic Controls |
| | Battery Connector | | Lights - Head and Tail |
| | Battery - Discharge Indicator | | Lights - Warning |
| | Belt | | Mast |
| | Brakes - Parking | | Oil Leaks |
| | Brakes - Service | | Oil Pressure |
| | Cables | | Overhead Guard |
| | Engine Oil Level | | Radiator Level |
| | Forks | | Safety Equipment |
| | Fuel | | Steering |
| | Gauges | | Tires |
| | Horn | | Unusual Noises |
| | Hoses | | Other _____ |

Notes:_____

_____

_____

_____

_____

_____

_____

_____

_____

Operator's Name:_____

Operator's Signature:_____

Supervisor's Name:_____

Supervisor's Signature:_____

Date: _____ Shift: _____

Truck Number:_____ Electric:____ Internal Combustion:____

Hour Meter Start:_____ End:_____ Total Hours:_____

Check any defective item and explain in the notes section below:

| | | | |
|---|---|---|---|
| | Accelerator | | Hour Meter |
| | Alarms | | Hydraulic Controls |
| | Battery Connector | | Lights - Head and Tail |
| | Battery - Discharge Indicator | | Lights - Warning |
| | Belt | | Mast |
| | Brakes - Parking | | Oil Leaks |
| | Brakes - Service | | Oil Pressure |
| | Cables | | Overhead Guard |
| | Engine Oil Level | | Radiator Level |
| | Forks | | Safety Equipment |
| | Fuel | | Steering |
| | Gauges | | Tires |
| | Horn | | Unusual Noises |
| | Hoses | | Other _____ |

Notes:_____

_____

_____

_____

_____

_____

_____

_____

_____

Operator's Name:_____

Operator's Signature:_____

Supervisor's Name:_____

Supervisor's Signature:_____

Made in the USA
Las Vegas, NV
28 September 2022

56105451R00111